INNOVATION AND CHANGE

MODERN EDUCATIONAL THOUGHT
Series Editor: Professor Andy Hargreaves,
                    Ontario Institute for Studies in Education

This important new series contains some of the very best of modern educational thought that will stimulate interest and controversy among teachers and educationalists alike.

It brings together writers of distinction and originality within educational studies who have made significant contributions to policy and practice. The writers are all scholars of international standing who are recognized authorities in their own particular field and who are still actively researching and advancing knowledge in that field.

The series represents some of their best and most distinctive writing as a set of provocative, interrelated essays addressing a specific theme of contemporary importance. A unique feature of the series is that each collection includes a critical introduction to the author's work written by another influential figure in the field.

Current titles:

Roger Dale: *The State and Education Policy*
Andy Hargreaves: *Curriculum and Assessment Reform*
Martyn Hammersley: *Classroom Ethnography*
Jean Rudduck: *Innovation and Change*

Forthcoming titles include:

Stephen Ball: *Education and Political Process*
Ivor Goodson: *Pupils, Pedagogy and Power*

Innovation and Change
Developing Involvement and Understanding

JEAN RUDDUCK

OPEN UNIVERSITY PRESS
Milton Keynes · Philadelphia

Open University Press
Celtic Court
22 Ballmoor
Buckingham
MK18 1XW

and

1900 Frost Road, Suite 101
Bristol, PA 19007, USA

First published 1991

British Library Cataloguing in Publication Data

Rudduck, Jean
    Innovation and change : developing involvement and understanding.
    – (Modern educational thought).
    1. Education. Innovation
    I. Title   II.Series
    370

    ISBN 0–335–09581–X
    ISBN 0–335–09580–1 (pbk)

Library of Congress Cataloging–in–Publication Data

Rudduck, Jean.
    Innovation and change : developing involvement and understanding /
Jean Rudduck.
        p.   cm. — (Modern educational thought)
    Includes bibliographical references (p.) and indexes.
    ISBN 0–335–09580–1 (pb).   ISBN 0–335–09581–X (hb)
    1. Educational innovations.   2. Student participation in
administration.   3. Teacher participation in administration.
    4. Group work in education.   I. Title.   II. Series.
    LB1027.R83   1990
    371.1'06 — dc20   90-7626
                                                                   CIP

Typeset by Inforum Typesetting, Portsmouth
Printed in Great Britain by St Edmundsbury Press, Bury St Edmunds, Suffolk

Contents

Acknowledgements

This book is based on work published over the last 7 years, although many of the ideas explored have their roots in earlier experiences. The sources for each chapter are listed below. In almost all cases, substantial modifications have been made.

Chapters

1   The first part is based on Rudduck, J. (1985). From projects to programmes: The view from the sharp end. In M. Plaskow (ed.), *The Life and Death of the Schools Council*, pp. 143–54. Lewes: Falmer Press.
2   Rudduck, J. (1986). *Understanding Curriculum Change*. USDE Papers in Education 6. Sheffield: University of Sheffield.
3   Rudduck, J. and Hopkins, D. (1984). *The Sixth Form and Libraries: Problems of Access to Knowledge*. Library and Information Research Report 24. London: British Library.
4   Mainly unpublished material, but reference is made to Cowie, H. and Rudduck, J. (1988). *Cooperative Group Work: An Overview* and *School and Classroom Studies* (Vols 1 and 2 of Learning Together, Working Together). London: BP Educational Service.
5   Rudduck, J. (1984). Introducing innovation to pupils. In D. Hopkins and M. Wideen (eds) *Alternative Perspectives on School Improvement*, pp. 53–66. Lewes: Falmer Press.
6   Rudduck, J. (1983). In-service courses for pupils as a basis for implementing curriculum change. *British Journal of In-service Education*, 10 (1), 32–42.
7   Rudduck, J. (1984). The 'hypothesis teacher' and the problem of helping children gain power through understanding. In B. Simon (ed.), *Margaret Gracie: A Teacher for our Time*, pp. 15–24 (printed privately).
8   Rudduck, J. (1988). The ownership of change as a basis for teachers' professional learning. In J. Calderhead (ed.), *Teachers' Professional Learning*, pp. 205–22. Lewes: Falmer Press.

9   Rudduck, J. (1985). The improvement of the art of teaching through research. *Cambridge Journal of Education*, 15 (3), 123–7.
10   Rudduck, J. (1987). Partnership supervision as a basis for the professional development of teachers. In M. Wideen and I. Andrews (eds) *Staff Development for School Improvement*, pp. 129–41. Lewes: Falmer Press.
11   Rudduck, J. and Wilcox, B. (1988). Issues of ownership and partnership in school-centred innovation. *Research Papers in Education*, 3 (3), 157–79.
12   Mainly unpublished material, but some passages draw on Rudduck, J. (1989). Practitioner research and programmes of initial teacher education. *Westminster Studies in Education*, 12, 61–72.

I am grateful to the copyright holders for permission to reproduce parts of the original versions: British Library Board (Chapter 3); CARFAX Publishing Company (Chapter 12); Falmer Press (Chapters 1, 5, 8, 10); NFER-Nelson (Chapter 11); Professor Brian Simon (Chapter 7); the editors of the *British Journal of In-service Education* (Chapter 6).

I am also grateful to my various writing partners for agreeing that I might refer to, or reproduce substantial parts of, papers or chapters that they have co-authored: Helen Cowie, David Hopkins and Brian Wilcox.

In the various chapters, I refer to a number of research or development projects and I would like to acknowledge my debt to the people that I have had the opportunity to work with over the years:

The Humanities Curriculum Project (1967–72).   A project funded by the Schools Council and the Nuffield Foundation and directed by Lawrence Stenhouse. Co-workers were John Elliott, John Hipkin, Maurice Plaskow. The evaluation team was led by Barry MacDonald and included Stephen Humble, Helen Simons and Gajendra Verma.

Man: A Course of Study (1972–78).   The British dissemination programme was jointly managed by Lawrence Stenhouse and myself with help from Marsden Bradshaw, Peter Coatham, Maggie Gracie, Lucila Haynes, Howard Hilton, Charles Townley and many others. Frances Link of Curriculum Development Associates, Washington, supported the initiative.

Introducing Innovation to Pupils (1979–81).   A project funded by the Social Science Research Council (now the Economic and Social Research Council). Charles Hull worked with me on this project.

Libraries, Academic Study and the Sixth Form (1979–82).   A project funded by the British Library and directed by Lawrence Stenhouse. The main co-workers were Beverley Labbett (co-ordinator) and John Cockburn; there was also a team of field workers. David Hopkins shared the task of writing the report.

Partnerships in Professional Development (1980–82).   An enquiry into partnership supervision in initial teacher training was initiated by Jim Chivas, a lecturer on secondment from a college in Australia; Alan Sigsworth and Jean Rudduck joined him in the enquiry. This led to a small project, funded by the Schools Council, to look at partnerships in in-service. The team included Nick May, Jean Rudduck, Alan Sigsworth and Roy Tamsett.

Cooperative Group Work (1985–89).   A project funded by British Petroleum. Helen Cowie worked with me on this project.

New Teaching Strategies in Biotechnology (1985–91).   A project funded by the Manpower Services Commission (now the Training Agency). Co-workers were Jenny Henderson (co-ordinator), Ross Cullen, Richard Goddard, Stephen Knutton, Vic Lally, Esther Parham and Judy Samuel.

Critical Introduction: From Innovation to Reform – A Framework for Analysing Change

BARRY MACDONALD

Innovation and change in education is the theme and central concern of this book, whose author has been, and continues to be, a prominent commentator on, and contributor to, the quest for a better quality of educational life for all those who are compelled by the state to spend 15 000 hours of their growth in the institutions we call schools.

For those of us in the West, perhaps particularly those of us in the UK and USA, the word 'innovation' already has a dated feel. It seems to belong to a chapter of our post-war history that has closed. Reform is now the banner headline of the politicians who have seized upon the alleged failure of the innovators so as to take control of the process of change and, in the UK at least, to make the central issue one of relations rather than relationships. There is an ambiguity in the rhetoric of the reformers that should not escape our notice, and that helps to explain why the most unlikely of bedfellows, elitists and egalitarians, can be found among their ranks. It is not always clear whether they are claiming to be able to achieve the same objectives as the innovators by more effective means, i.e. crudely speaking by the exercise of power, or whether the allegation is that innovation has been successful but regressive, so that what is required is a restoration of former virtues that are threatened by abuses introduced and fostered by meddling and muddle-headed professionals. The point is important – indeed it is crucial – because it turns upon the issue of the impact of the innovation movement over the past three or four decades. This is the issue I wish to address.

The time is opportune. There has been a great deal of hand-wringing of late (see Fullan, 1989, for the latest instance) about the various inadequacies of the various strategies of change that have been devised and employed to cajole, seduce or pressurize schools into doing better by their charges, all such strategies fit only for consignment to the dustbin of history. The gloom is pervasive, the sense of impotence understandable as the space vacated by the self-incriminating pathologists of the innovation bubble is filled by those whose educational obligations are less compelling than their political imperatives. Jean

Rudduck's account is hardly of this ilk, although her nostalgia for the false dawn of the 1960s and her somewhat downbeat conclusion do give the impression of a terminal decline of the prospects for the kind of professional, communal and fraternal culture that is the core of her advocacy. In this she is far from being alone, either in her pessimism, or in her conviction that the civil rights to educational opportunity at least partially realized by the raising of the school leaving age in 1972 can only be converted into intellectual rights by the development of a collaborative culture of schooling based on respect for persons.

That there is a long way to go can hardly be denied – black children are every day denied those rights and that respect in schools up and down the country, truancy among the recently enfranchised is on the increase, the proportion of poor people's children entering higher education has not risen in 40 years. That the current legislative framework is hostile to such a culture is publicly denied but cannot seriously be doubted: the Education Reform Act of 1988 promises the restoration of stratification in all its forms on a bogus notion of merit and choice – the social segregation of schools, the reification of streaming, greater differentiation of roles and rewards for school personnel, and the standardization of curriculum and performance assessment to disguise the distributive injustice of economic selection. It's a 'fixed' market, driven by the values of possessive individualism and negative interdependence, a competition in which the winners are known in advance, the losers left with only their own apparent shortcomings to blame. It is the economic liberal's revenge on the 'permissive' 1960s (in this perspective, denunciation replaces nostalgia) and in particular on the comprehensive school.

Yes, it is difficult to be optimistic in such circumstances but it is not impossible, as I hope to demonstrate. In doing so, I have to say that my remarks are not assumed to have global application. They are confined to one case, one country, one experience of post-war educational development through the medium of systematic innovation. I leave to others the more problematic task of extrapolation.

The getting of wisdom

Any collection of chapters, such as those that follow this Introduction, runs the risk of demarcating the trees at the expense of the reader's grasp of the wood, which may remain implicit or subject to only fleeting glimpses in passing. Although the author in this case has minimized the risk by writing pieces specifically for this publication and by careful editing of previously published items, the risk is still evident, particularly for readers who may come to this book with a sketchy knowledge of the context in which the kinds of understandings and insights displayed by the author were developed. In choosing only her most recent works for inclusion, the evolution of understanding is understated, although its roots in the past are stressed by the author herself.

It may be helpful, therefore, if I offer a brief depiction of the learning curve that lies behind these accounts of innovative experimentation. Although I know the author well, I would not presume to offer this in the sense of a personal profile, but rather as a generalized summary of professional learning about the possibilities and the conditions of school improvement on the part of those, like Jean, whose continuous involvement over a long period of time in a significant educational movement has been marked by perceptual leaps and strategic adaptations as the complexity of the task unfolded.

It is very difficult for those outside the schools to improve the quality of provision within them. That we now know. Twenty-five years ago, we thought differently. We thought then that the combination of money and good ideas, invested in external agencies, would quickly and easily transform our schools in line with the post-war transformation of our economy and our social life. It was not to be. There are no easy solutions. As Jean Rudduck points out, it was not enough, as we discovered in the 1960s, to supply teachers with better books and packaged pedagogies, although good materials and supportive advice do matter. It is the quality of the teachers themselves and the nature of their commitment to change that determines the quality of teaching and the quality of school improvement. Teachers are, on the whole, poor implementers of other people's ideas. Teacher development therefore – and this is one of the main themes of her writing – is a precondition of curriculum development, and teachers must play a generative role in the development of better curricula. Their understanding, their sense of responsibility, their commitment to the effective delivery of educational experience for their pupils, is significantly enhanced when they own the ideas and author the means by which ideas are translated into classroom practice.

This finding, now commonplace within the professional culture, but very slow to crystallize and emerge from the first decade of national curriculum reform, had its major impact on the in-service education of teachers in the 1970s. While the government continued to pursue national initiatives, varying their approach in a search for the optimum combination of central prescription and grassroots initiative, many of the large number of individuals who had played central roles in curriculum development projects set about a different strategy based on this finding. Throughout the 1970s, in-service education became a revitalized source of curriculum change, where the concept of a new kind of teacher, the fully fledged 'professional', was increasingly nurtured. While pre-service educators continued to emphasize established competences, in-service tutors began to equip teachers to engage in the curriculum research, development and evaluation activities that during the previous decade had been the domain of the specialist. The 'teacher as researcher' and the 'action research classroom' were prominent among the slogans that energized the new phase of intervention that operated without *ad-hoc* central government support, which continued to emphasize content priorities through categorical funding.

From that period, as a result of some of the difficulties of engaging individual teachers in the process of curriculum development, emerged another important insight. Partly, admittedly, as a consequence of the growing accountability movement, which put pressure on schools to be more accountable to their constituencies, but due also in no small measure to a realization that the professionalization of teachers had implications for the organizational form of the institutions in which they worked, a further shift of thinking took place. It became clear that the unit of teacher development ought to be the school. Individual teachers could not get very far without running up against the constraints of collective practice and institutional habits. As we entered the 1980s, new notions of school-based self-review, self-evaluation and self-development became more prominent in curriculum planning and innovation theory.

There were, then, essentially three main stages (and I am here formalizing and making explicit the different sequences of experience and insight presented in this book): from package development to teacher development to school development. But there were other lessons from the experience of curriculum development. These lessons had to do with levels and locations of decision making, and about the spread of ideas and practices. In general, it was concluded that local enterprise is more likely to improve quality than national enterprise, especially as local support had proved to be much more important in achieving change than had been initially assumed, and psychological support just as essential as material support. National authorities, it seemed, should set policy in broad terms, but leave localities to mediate and modify in the light of local needs, and invite schools and teachers to invent appropriate curriculum responses. This would maximize the deployment of talent, spread the sense of ownership, and allow a needed flexibility within a given range of tolerance. The relationship between participants in the curriculum development enterprise will be more effective if it derives from the notion of a professional, diversely accountable community rather than from linear, hierarchical direction. During the 1970s, spurred by a growing sense of disappointment in curriculum reform efforts and a demand for a better knowledge of schooling on which to base new strategies, there was a great deal of research and evaluation that focused closely upon attempts to identify the conditions under which better schooling might be achieved. One clear and consistent implication of this research was the need to take account of particular circumstances, varying between schools as well as between localities, in planning for improvement. Jean Rudduck's distinctive contribution here was to underline the importance of pupils' responses to what they experienced as 'imposed' change: she urged teachers, bearing in mind the conditions of recent curriculum history in their schools, to try to bring pupils in on the logics of school and classroom policies for change. With regard to the spread of ideas, it was also noted that lateral rather than vertical lines of communication are more effective in transmitting ideas and practices, a point of considerable relevance to the concept of teacher, school and community collaboration.

Finally, to complete this thumbnail sketch of innovation theory, there was support for the view that the degree of professional autonomy implicit in some of these recommendations could only be justified if it was matched by a professional commitment to public accountability and responsiveness to public critique. The work of professionals must be open to public influence and informed public judgement.

This getting of wisdom seems in retrospect to have been painfully slow, and will still seem to many to be woefully inadequate, imbued from start to finish with political and sociological naivety. There are worse crimes, but those liberal humanists who engaged the system and sought to mend its ways had to suffer a lot of sniping from the sidelines, especially from the new sociologists of education, whose dominance/submission certainties tended to mock the very notion of engagement, let alone to decry the evolving focus of the innovators as teacher protectionism. But they too have enjoyed a learning curve. In *Education and Power* (1982), Michael Apple argues powerfully for agency and involvement in concrete, not just theoretic work: 'It is at the level of our daily lives where the cultural, political and economic spheres are lived out in all their complexity and contradictions . . .' In summarizing the learning of the innovators, I have confined myself to those learnings of direct utility to the discretion and opportunities available to them. I shall return later to the issue of political consciousness.

Careers and continuity

The chapters in this book chart the course of a professional biography in England from the early 1960s to the late 1980s. Jean Rudduck began that period as a classroom teacher and finished it as a university professor. So did I, and so did many others whose careers in education were carved out of the opportunity structure that opened up as the innovation industry recast the credentials of personal advance. It is amusing now to recall, from those early days, some anxiety expressed to me by officials of the Schools Council about the future prospects of their project directors. Plucked from nowhere by an unsystematic trawling procedure on the part of entrepreneurial administrators who took for granted the need to manipulate the clumsy bureaucracy of innovation that embodied the political settlement of the time, these men and women 'of ideas' were then basking in the limelight of national attention, the epicentre of the centre-periphery model. But what was to happen to them after their 2, 3 or 5 years of curriculum messiahship were over? Would they be left to pack up their tents and return to whence they came? Hardly a fair return for the leading edge protégés of patronage, let alone a sensible response to the need to conserve and keep on tap a new and valued commodity – expertise in curriculum development.

Keep in mind that very few of those involved had been drawn from the university sector. There was no equivalent here of the 'leading scholar' approach in the USA, whereby it was hoped that the prestige and authority of the curriculum package would ensure an easy passage to the classroom. In England, it was largely the lower reaches of the education system that constituted the recruiting grounds of innovation – the colleges of teacher training and the schools themselves. For these upwardly mobile but academically underqualified recruits, there was no ready-made entry into the discipline-based heights of the institutional order. The universities had not been party to the political settlement that saw the ministry, the local authorities and the teacher unions sink their differences over curriculum control in the tri-partite Schools Council.

Thus it was that the patrons and minders of the early innovators, or at least of the more eminent members thereof, saw the need to secure a future for them. Wheels turned and deals were struck. One of them led to the setting up of the Centre for Applied Research in Education (CARE) at the University of East Anglia, which (and this was thought to be a blessing at the time) had no school of education. This kind of package deal (tenured university posts for four people who didn't have two PhDs to rub together) implanted in higher education the seeds of its reconstruction – in my view, the totally unintended but most significant and lasting impact of the curriculum development movement. Had it depended on the negotiating power of the Schools Council (the bait dangled before the universities was the promise of continued Council funding at a point in time when they were beginning to sense the coming financial squeeze), then the impact would have been limited. Outfits like CARE would have remained, as they were initially seen, as paying guests in an otherwise indifferent establishment. But in fact the anxieties felt by project managers were to prove utterly misplaced.

The curriculum development projects of the 1960s (by the end of the decade some 200 national initiatives had been funded) led, in the 1970s, to a restaffing of a still expanding system (the school leaving age was raised to 16 in 1972) on a new basis – the experience of change. It was not only the schools that sniffed the spoor of government favour or sensed the threat of marginalization posed by a new and independent industry within their domain. The scenario that then unfolded is not without its irony, as the bruised and battered veterans of what was already being seen as a massive failure at classroom level began to reap the rich career rewards of their endeavours. They poured into the departments of education in the universities and the polytechnics, the local authority advisory services, even the national inspectorate and senior school positions, bringing to their new responsibilities a hands-on knowledge of the practice of schooling that would breathe new life into those atrophied institutions by challenging their traditions and offering them a new role. The beachheads of an unfamiliar academic territory were rapidly established in higher education, increasingly under the title of 'curriculum studies'. The theoretical tradition of education based on derivative disciplines began to give way to the new theorists of educational practice whose theory was based on the close observation of new curricula in action, grounded theory of school life whose conceptual catholicity and seemingly casual disregard for the carefully constructed authority of the social sciences had to meet and survive accusations of amateurism and naive ignorance. But survive and flourish they did, not least because, supported by their colleagues in the local authority advisory services, they exerted an increasingly decisive role in the reshaping of in-service education for teachers, taking that opportunity to draw their students into the process of field-based enquiry into school problems and practices. That opportunity was extended as more and more colleges of initial training were incorporated into the institutions of higher education.

So when Jean Rudduck writes in the later pages of this book about the important need for continuing the partnership between higher education staff and teachers and student teachers, what gives meaning to her concerns and explains her aspirations is, I think, the historical location – in higher education settings – of the curriculum innovators and their camp followers (the curriculum evaluators), with all their close-up understanding of the process of change in schools and school systems. Their own 'logic in use' offered an upstart challenge to the reconstructed logic of the social sciences – long dominant in departments of education – which had assumed and emulated the natural sciences in their search for a parallel form of objectivity-based certainty. ˙

It was in this context that the curriculum innovators and the evaluators at the time, and for the most part largely innocent of these seismic rumblings in the groves of academe, engaged in the unholy methodological improvisation that came to characterize their pursuit of useful knowledge in the circumstances of innovative action. They were helped, at least initially, by a sponsoring establishment of civil servants, themselves the product of a gifted amateur tradition, pragmatically inclined and dismissive in any case of the utility of university-based research practices. They had to invent a research they could do. And, when finally they carried that research baggage into the commanding heights of the system, they found more fertile ground for legitimacy than they could possibly have ancitipated.

I am aware as I write of giving an exaggerated impression of the impact at this level, an impression of transformation that would not be substantiated by detailed documentation of practice across the country. What would be difficult to exaggerate is the responsiveness of students to the new style courses, whether these students are experienced teachers whose known scepticism about the value of their initial training is rooted in its failure to address the theory/practice divide, or whether they are more assorted groups of aspirants to academic honours who increasingly demand the opportunity to employ the methodologies of field-based enquiry in pursuit of research credentials. One index of the change in client orientation is the fact that in the early 1980s, at a national conference of research degree supervisors organized by the British Educational Research Association, one of the major concerns expressed by those in attendance was the difficulty of supervising students who wanted to do research that could not readily be confined within the single discipline frameworks in which many of their supervisors were qualified.

The result was that, far from being inducted as novitiates into the exclusive realms of discipline membership as the price of admission, and thus detaching themselves from the theatre of practical action, the Curriculum Innovators found themselves free, not only to continue their mission, and not only to apply their wisdom through an avenue (teacher development) that corresponded with their perception of need, but also to construct a new authority for the extension of formal knowledge construction – the building of a multi-professional researching community – to those who had formerly been confined to the role of research consumption. I have no doubt that the crisis of confidence in the social sciences contributed substantially to the democratization of the right to research that flowed from the influx of the innovators into the universities in the early and mid-1970s. I am not, of course, denying for one moment that the currently dominant political ideology has checked the advance of these important gains, and continues to do its utmost not only to restore but to stratify even further the traditional research establishment. What I am saying is that the alternative tradition has taken root, will not go away, and is sustained by student demand. The innovators who began in the classrooms have now penetrated the institutional order and are beginning to reshape the infrastructure of schooling.

Failure revisited

We seem to have forgotten something. It takes 50 years for a new social practice to become widely established. So concluded Miles in 1964, at a point when the problem of curriculum obsolescence had already led to substantial federal investment in the USA in the fledgling innovation industry and in the UK to the setting up of the Schools Council for Curriculum and Examinations. What's more, added Miles, we don't know much about the process or how to accelerate it. Miles' book, *Innovation in Education*, was much admired and totally ignored. Would-be innovators, both before and after his sobering reflections, have been lucky to get 5 years to accomplish the job. It isn't enough.

Why 5 years? I remember asking a senior civil servant who chaired the steering committee of a national curriculum initiative, 'What does the Minister want to know about the Programme?' He replied, 'Two things. Will the Programme transform education? Will the Programme transform education before the next election?' Political time-frames are short in electoral democracies and the need to show quick results is a paramount condition of investment.

After three decades of attempts at the quick educational fix (see p. 30), a period during which this preoccupation with the development of schooling has become widely shared by countries around the globe, we should not be surprised that in 1989 Michael Fullan should pronounce that 'All reform efforts to date have failed.' Although he bases this conclusion largely on North American experiences, many school-watchers around the world would nod their heads in substantial agreement (Jean Rudduck quotes some on pp. 26–7). The post-war experience of systematic attempts to improve the quality of educational provision has been a history of failure, at least in terms of meeting short-term professional hopes and political expectations.

Of course 'improvement' and 'transformation' are value-loaded concepts whose meanings are both temporally and contextually unstable. Social concerns fluctuate, ideologies rise and fall. Because schooling is assumed to shape minds as well as competences, it is a battleground for competing visions of how social 'goods' (in both senses of the term) should be realized, distributed and protected. Education is both a moral and a technical discourse. Engineers and philosophers vie with elitists and egalitarians for a piece of the action that sets the framework within which teachers deliver their service to the young. Magnates keep a watchful, and parents a fearful, eye on the proceedings.

What does it mean, in this context, to say that all reforms have failed? It means something very precise. It means that no form of substantive discontent (with the quality or suitability of curriculum provision) that is sufficiently influential to attract publicly funded *ad-hoc* remediation has been eliminated, or even diminished, by targeted intervention. Jean Rudduck uses different words, but the import is the same: the curriculum interventions did not manage, on the whole, to engage with the 'deep structures' of schooling that hold habits and values in place. But at other levels too, the curriculum development movement was seen as having failed to deliver. The result, at least in the USA and UK, is a marked shift in control and legitimacy from the professionals to the politician, in strategy from facilitation to coercion, and in vision from an expansionist to a reductionist view of schooling. In the USA, the federal government, constitutionally restricted to a policy of investment-led voluntarism, has largely withdrawn from direct involvement in school improvement, to be replaced by prescriptive state centrism. In the UK, the teacher-dominated Schools Council has been closed, a national curriculum introduced for the first time, and a system of criterion-referenced achievement tests is being added to the traditional public examinations to assure compliance, productivity and accountability.

An economic model of schooling, and its evaluative correlate the performance indicator, is now firmly entrenched. Schools have annual targets, managed workforces, and an ideal of 'effectiveness' to aspire to. There is no place for curriculum development or variation. Standardization is a prerequisite of competitive comparison, performance replaces provision as the basis of consumer judgement and market choice.

Now let us compare that 'outcome' of 30 years with the original agenda of the Schools Council. These extracts are taken from Working Paper 2, *Raising the School Leaving Age*:

> The problem is to give every man some access to a complex cultural inheritance, some hold on his personal life and on his relationships with the various communities to which he belongs, some extension of his understanding of, and sensitivity towards, other human beings. The aim is to forward understanding, discrimination and judgement in the human field – it will involve reliable factual knowledge, where this is appropriate, direct experience, imaginative experience, some appreciation of the dilemmas of the human condition, of the rough-hewn nature of many of our institutions, and some rational thought about them. (Schools Council, 1965, para. 60)

> All of this may seem to some teachers like a programme for people who have both mental ability and maturity beyond the reach of most who will leave at the age of sixteen. The Council, however, thinks it is important not to assume that this is so, but rather to probe by experiment in the classroom how far ordinary pupils can be taken. (Schools Council, 1965, para. 61)

Not all of the curriculum missionaries let loose by Schools Council sponsor-
ship in the 1960s set out with that agenda, and few put it seriously to the test.
One of those who did, and whose 'experiment' in the classroom evoked a
passionate responsiveness in teachers fed up with the deadening routine and the
moral vacuum of their occupational practice, was the late Lawrence Stenhouse,
the acknowledged inspiration of the work reported in this book. I was in
charge of the evaluation of the Humanities Curriculum Project. A few years
ago, I was asked to provide a summary comment on the project for a book
concerned with pupil perspectives on schooling (Schostak and Logan, 1984). I
wrote as follows:

> At the core of Lawrence Stenhouse's Humanities Curriculum Project
> was quite a radical proposition – that quite ordinary kids were capable of
> the kind of intellectual life historically achieved by a small elite. The
> problem was how to release them from the contrary and self-fulfilling
> assumption embodied in institutional and pedagogic practice. The pro-
> ject did this by promoting a style of classroom discussion in which the
> proactive role of the teacher and the reactive role of the pupils was
> reversed – the teachers were forced to shut up and listen, and the pupils
> to move into the vacuum. Both were deskilled, both found themselves
> starting from scratch. Most of them couldn't stand the strain, and soon
> relapsed. Some made quite remarkable breakthroughs. I vividly recall one
> occasion when a conference of very senior personnel in the education
> system was introduced to the project via a videotape I had made of a
> group discussion in a secondary modern school. The discussion was of
> such quality that some of those present simply refused to believe that this
> was a group of so-called Newsom children. But that was Stenhouse's
> point, and in my view there were enough instances of this kind to suggest
> that the kind of teaching young people usually get and the kind of
> learning of which they are capable may be mutually exclusive activities.

There is ample evidence in the chapters that follow to support Stenhouse's
proposition – and my thesis about the gap between potential and the realization
of that potential. What is clear is that contemporary political prescriptions of
the form and function of schooling does not bear analysis in these terms, but
rather constitute a denial of both the aspirations and the possibilities they
reveal. I have argued, however, that increasingly sophisticated notions of the
kind of schooling that could realistically advance such aspirations are alive and
well in the British system, that they constitute a thriving counter-culture, and
that they are ready to make a comeback when the extraordinary political
regime under which we now labour is dead and buried. I base this view on an
unintended effect of a policy decision taken by the Schools Council in its early
days. This decision is referred to by Stenhouse (1980) himself in these terms:

> As I interpret it, the Schools Council was generally hostile to the designa-
> tion of curriculum development as a professional area: that is, it did not
> encourage directors to undertake successive development projects or to

regard themselves as career curriculum specialists. This was associated with its general policy of seconding teachers to staff curriculum development teams.

The Council could not remotely have foreseen that such a policy would carry a practice-oriented culture of enquiry, theory and development into the far reaches of the professional system and fundamentally disrupt its compartmentalization.

The impetus of the movement in this phase helped to transform both the focus and the methodology of educational research (reinforced no doubt by the availability of new microtechnology and by the renaissance of ethnographic sociology), creating the basis for an educational theory of educational practice. Teacher education began to take on a more collaborative, active and investigative character concerned with school-based problem solving rather than theoretic sophistication or familiarization with the latest curriculum trends. I would hazard that the popularity of this change with its clientele can in part be attributed to the impact of the curriculum development phase on teacher culture, the process dynamics generated by its forms and values, the widespread experience of participation that at its height was offered to teachers and schools. Although the curriculum materials and pedagogies that resulted from such collaboration were not widely adopted (and hence the accusation of failure), that experience was both valued (as well as valuable in career terms) for the thousands of teachers involved.

These are consequences of great import, particularly within as 50-year perspective. In so far as House (1974) is correct in asserting that the school is an institution 'frozen' in the order of the institutions, this thawing of its own immediately embracing institutions could reasonably be seen as a necessary if insufficient precondition of school improvement.

There are, of course, other institutions, some barely mentioned to this point. Schools are, as we know, political constructions, constrained by economic doctrines, powerful interests, organized ideologies. Professionals act on licence, under varying conditions that define the extent to which they can fulfil their 'implicit' contract. If Hamilton (1989) is right in claiming that schooling is simultaneously a site of social regulation and a site of social redefinition, it is time now to turn to the backcloth of political regulation against which the drama of the innovation movement has been played out.

We, the innovators, began under benign and supportive government and saw the problem largely as a technical one, under professional control. Along the way, as economic failure put an end to the bi-partisan educational expansionism of successive governments and to political detachment from the management of schooling, we have become politicized as we have become marginalized. This is just as well, as it has helped us to understand the limits of what can be accomplished by schools alone, and to get a better sense of what else has to change before schools can.

In this sense, Thatcherism (and I think I may have created some sort of record by not mentioning the lady's name until now) has been particularly helpful. Her seemingly effortless dismantling of an assumed democracy has politicized all of us, and revealed how fragile and inadequate are the checks and balances we fondly believe protect us against what one of her own ministers called an 'electoral dictatorship'. Words like 'dominance' and 'reproduction' now have a much wider currency in educational discourse as an enforced, non-negotiable and educationally indefensible model of schooling gets underway.

The development of a political consciousness in education was delayed by 30 years. The post-war expansion of schooling was powered by a political consensus around the notion of Keynesian social democracy (Marquand, 1988). Throughout that period, it seemed that economic buoyancy would finance the agreed goals of full employment, adequate social services, and the co-existence of public and private enterprise. In 1970, expenditure on education exceeded expenditure on defence for the first, but last time. The writing was now on the wall (and the Schools Council under severe political attack as the warning signs were taken heed of) and recession looming. The consensus collapsed under Labour in the mid- to late-1970s in a massive failure of adaptation to the new economic realities. The truce was over, as was the indulgence. The politics of moderation were out, the politics of extremism in. The sense of a failing society (with schooling, of course, a favourite target) was pervasive, and of a failing socialism, conclusive. In an extraordinary ideological coup (not least of her own party), Thatcher seized the opportunity to introduce and implement a version of economic liberalism not seen since the nineteenth century – the undistorted market. That she has remained in power for a record period of continuity in office, winning three successive elections in the process, is testimony to the persuasiveness of conviction politics in a society that has lost its way, to her ruthless command of party allegiance, and her exploitation of the unrestrained power that our form of democracy offers even a government chosen by a minority of its citizens.

As Margaret Archer's (1984) historical and structural comparison of state educational systems implies, only the maximization of state power and its unconditional application could possibly have achieved in a decentralized system like the UK the degree of systematized uniformity that is now embodied in the legislative framework of schools. Archer characterizes such systems as unresponsive to central manipulation, subject to internal disjuncture, but offering multiple opportunities for internal innovation to their professional networks. The question then is, what happens next? The legislation has still to be substantially implemented, the networks largely hostile, the Thatcher government tottering as its over-reach begins to hit the 'haves' as well as the 'have nots'. Marquand (1988) argues that neo-liberalism will fail for the same reasons as neo-socialism failed in the 1970s, because they both lack the basis of a moral appeal beyond individual or sectional interests. He foresees (optimistically) their succession by the politics of negotiation, interests moderated by an acceptance of the common good.

Well, forecasting is a tricky business, and events make fools of those who venture. At this point in time, with Mandela out, the 'Wall' down, and the military/industrial complex reeling from its first major setback since the

Second World War, I hesitate to stick my neck out. To be sure Thatcher will go. I'd like to think she will flounder on the bedrock of our biological sociability, but suspect her economics will bring a reckoning first. With respect to this book and what it has to say, I would like to see the emergence of a new political framework in which, to the discourse about liberty and equality, is added a discourse and a practice that is about fraternity. That is what this book, and the practices it describes, are essentially about, the conditions of community. And these are the conditions under which schooling might – just might – become educational for all its inhabitants.

Schooling cannot deliver us from poverty in all its forms, but these forms are interrelated, and schooling can do more than Coleman (1966) concluded. To deny the agency of the school is to deny the possibility of change, and to ignore the evidence.

References

Apple, M.W. (1982). *Education and Power*. Boston: Routledge and Kegan Paul.
Archer, M.S. (1984). *Social Origins of Educational Systems*. London: Sage.
Coleman, J. (1966). *Equality of Educational Opportunity*. The Coleman Report. Washington, D.C.: US Government Department of Health, Education and Welfare.
Fullan, M. (1989). Linking Classrooms and School Improvement. Invited Address, American Educational Research Association, San Francisco.
Hamilton, D. (1989). *Towards a Theory of Schooling*. Lewes: Falmer Press.
House, E. (1974). *The Politics of Educational Innovation*. Berkeley, Calif.: McCutchan.
Marquand, D. (1988). *The Unprincipled Society*. London: Fontana.
Miles, M.B. (ed.) (1964). *Innovation in Education*. New York: Columbia Teachers' College.
Schools Council (1965). *Raising the School Leaving Age*. Working Paper 2. London: Schools Council.
Schostak, J. and Logan, T. (1984). *Pupil Experience*. London: Croom Helm.
Stenhouse, L. (1980). *Curriculum Research and Development in Action*. London: Heinemann Educational.

PART 1

Setting the Scene

1 Getting Hooked on Change: An Autobiographical Note

> Sometimes a landscape seems to be less a setting for the life of its inhabitants than a curtain behind which their struggles, achievements and accidents take place.
>
> For those who, with the inhabitants, are behind the curtain, landmarks are no longer only geographic but also biographical and personal. (Berger and Mohr, 1967)

Since the late 1960s, there have been massive swings of mood and major changes of direction in education. All of us who were actively involved then in research and development have looked out on the landscape of change, but we will have experienced it and responded to it differently. The chapters in this book record the continuities of concern than have defined my professional perspective.

Getting hooked

It all started, I think, with an inspection of the school where I was teaching. The Inspector for English seemed to enjoy what was happening in the classroom – although I can remember only one swirling, frenetically participatory exploration of the Pied Piper of Hamelin – and shortly after (the two events may not, of course, have been related) I received an invitation to an international conference for young teachers. There, as often happens at conferences, I lost my professional innocence: there were worlds outside the classroom that I had not dreamed of where fundamental educational ideas were examined and disputed, and where experiences were shared and criticized in a spirit of intellectual excitement and commitment that was new to me. After the conference, I was as bewildered as Bottom the Weaver: 'The eye of man hath not heard, the ear of man hath not seen, man's hand is not able to taste, his tongue to conceive nor his heart to report what my dream was.'

I had been a lively teacher with good classroom control and a delight in and respect for my subject, and would have succeeded for a few years on the energy and optimism of youth, but I had no real foundation of professional under-standing that could have carried me dynamically and effectively into mid-career. That is not such an uncommon situation, and what teachers like me look to then are the staged novelties of posts of special responsibility which can, sadly, prevent the deepening of pedagogic insight by offering incentives to move up the managerial ladder. My teacher training course had provided me with the basics, but basics are never enough: the training failed to equip me with ways of looking at and thinking about the events and interactions of the classroom as a basis for the improvement of my art as a teacher. Having sloughed off the thin skin of theory that I prudently acquired as protection against the summer examinations, I had no impulse to continue with the formal study of education, and I had no framework which could lead me to question my own implicit assumptions or that explained the workings of my own small world. And then, one day, shortly after attending the international conference, I applied for a job at the newly established Schools Council for Curriculum and Examinations – and was offered it. In such ways are promising teachers lured from the secure island of their school and – also like Bottom the Weaver – translated. The curriculum development movement was of course to be another translator of classroom teachers, a sort of Trojan Horse in reverse. I did not go back to the classroom.

The Schools Council had advertised for young teachers to form a research team under the leadership of Philip Taylor (who all too soon deserted us for the Chair in Education at Birmingham). It took a long time for the Council to work out – having decided that it was proper to have a research team – what to do with it. We had no real research experience and were given no research training, but we knew that policies were evolving and a certain sense of privilege at being part of something new enabled us to cope with our role uncertainties. We were linked to a number of enterprises that were relevant to the Council's developing understanding of its own educational agenda and aspirations. For instance, I visited the North West Regional Development Group where, under Alan Rudd's careful and encouraging leadership, teach-ers in different subject areas, across schools, met regularly to work out their own courses of study using the then novel framework of Bloom's Taxonomy of Educational Objectives (later I became a renegade and handed out car stickers that said 'Help Stamp Out Behavioural Objectives'). I was impressed by the support for collaborative planning that the objectives model offered and recognized the power and fruitfulness of working through teacher groups.

The work that I valued most was with the Government Social Survey, which led to the publication of *Enquiry 1: Young School Leavers* (Schools Coun-cil, 1968). I took part in pilot interviews and in the structuring of interview schedules. My involvement in *Enquiry 1* was important because it focused my serious attention on the importance of trying to understand pupils' perspectives on schooling.

There was, at this time, an air of speculative adventure and the climate was receptive to individuals with vision. We had our own internal charismatic figures. One afternoon, on the second anniversary of the Council's birthday, Derek Morrell, one of the joint secretaries, called all the staff together in a large bay-windowed room and addressed us. Our research team secretary commented: 'He makes you believe in it even if you don't understand what it's all about.' That was true. We entrusted the future to the joint secretaries – Derek Morrell, later Geoffrey Caston and Joslyn Owen. These were people whom you respected and whose visions you waited, patiently, to share.

The contracts of the research team were short-term. After 2 years, I took up a post at Brighton College of Education. I remember dropping my letter of application into the pillar box in London and then trying awkwardly to retrieve it. The post was in English, not in Education, and in many ways it was a wrong move. I continued to tie up work I had been doing for the Council while I was there and, after about 7 months, as I sat in my bleak black-and-white linoleum-floored study, one of the joint secretaries rang me and asked whether I would consider applying for the post of schools liaison officer on the Humanities Curriculum Project (HCP), a large-scale project which was to be funded as part of the Council's programme of curriculum development in preparation for the raising of the statutory school leaving age. The feasibility study was carried out while I was at the Council and its approach had not attracted me. 'No', I said. 'Why not go up for an interview?' he said. 'Well, it's a free trip to London', I thought, so I went – and in a sense I never came back.

Lawrence Stenhouse, the project's director, collected me in an old green Jaguar car from the railway station. Geoffrey Caston moved courteously to the back seat. No small talk: they continued their discussion, ignoring me. My resistance was intensifying! Lawrence interviewed me in a coffee bar, and all doubts evaporated! This was another man of vision: articulate, inspiring and confident. Again, I did not understand or grasp the significance of what he was about, but I responded to his values and to his commitment. I joined the HCP team. My responsibility was to forge links between the team, schools and local education authorities (LEAs). This was when I learned most about education. I was now part of a team which had a task, which had money to meet the needs of the task, and which had time to think about the task. Each week the HCP team took a whole day for a full staff meeting. This seemed at first an unpardonable extravagance given the demands that schools were making of us, but it was the time spent in discussion that gave us, over time, a shared understanding, and that provided a supportive forum for the intellectual and practical uncertainties that we were confronting. We learned to trust each other, and this proved important given the battering that we were to face, individually and as a group, as a result of the project's challenge to the established order of things.

The project was structured to reflect Lawrence Stenhouse's belief (1983b, p. 1) that 'the virtue of humanity is diminished in man when judgement is overruled by authority'. He defined the 'most civilised state' as the one whose 'citizens are successfully trusted with the responsibility of judgement'. He aspired to this responsibility both for the teachers and for students in schools: he wanted teachers to act as 'instruments for a redistribution of the means of autonomy and judgement'. The focus for our project was the study of human issues that are of universal concern to members of society: 'for example, abortion, divorce, the roles of men and women in society, streaming by ability in schools, war and pacifism, nuclear weapon production, etc' (Elliott, 1983, p. 112). These issues are drawn from 'areas of experience which are inherently controversial and where society acknowledges the right of individuals to disagree and exercise their own judgement' (ibid.).

The aim of the project (see Rudduck, 1988a) was to help pupils develop an understanding of social situations and human acts and the controversial value issues they raise. Taking aim and content together, the task for the project team was to create a strategy for handling controversial issues in the classroom. Stenhouse and Elliott argued that if controversy characterizes the content of the curriculum, then instructional teaching is inappropriate. The teaching style must be one that supports the exploration of evidence in the pursuit of understanding. If pupils are to arrive at a sense of responsibility for action, then they must be sure that the judgement that determines action is based on careful weighing of evidence and sensitive consideration of different perspectives. They have to realize that in the complex arenas of social action, answers cannot be dictated but must be constructed responsibly by individuals. The process of construction is fostered by dialogue that is questioning, critical, but essentially cooperative. Through such dialogue, the individual learns how to manage the task of looking at issues from different angles – a task that he or she may at times have to manage alone in adult life, without the support that fellow questioners provide in the classroom.

Thus, the project made a major contribution to the debate about knowledge and control in education as well as to the debate about the structure of curriculum development. The development projects were advancing along relatively untravelled paths: in addition to developing a coherent experimental pedagogy, we were discovering, documenting and analysing problems in the relationship between central team and pilot schools; problems of curriculum implementation; problems of materials production and censorship; problems of evaluating within a non-objectives model of curriculum development; and problems of designing and managing training workshops for teachers that were process-oriented and not materials-dominated. The Council's policy was wise: they gave us our head and they gave us support. This was the best way to proceed, for in those pioneering days the Council could only learn about curriculum development by observing and reflecting on what its project teams did.

The Schools Council was still deeply involved in the questions which the project was exploring at the time when our first phase of funding came to an end in 1970. It was also facing the dilemma of what to do about project teams when projects came to an end. Institutionalization in higher education was one answer. Opponents of the institutionalization principle argued, with some justification, that people with such experience and insight should get back into classrooms as soon as possible and try to lift it from the roots. The Council's joint secretaries in fact started negotiations to place the HCP team in a university setting and we moved to establish a new group at the University of East Anglia, the Centre for Applied Research in Education (CARE). Posts were offered to a core of people whose presence on the project was required right up to 1972 and who wished to stay on: Lawrence Stenhouse, Barry MacDonald, John Elliott and myself. The four of us, although officially tenured, accepted the fact that after 1972 we would be expected to find our own salaries out of research and development grants (a situation that continued until we launched a teaching programme and justified our presence in terms of student numbers).

Recognizing the agenda

Looking back in 1990, it seems that most of the ideas I have subsequently explored through research or curriculum development have their roots in the HCP. Three powerful images have dominated my thinking. One is the idea of pupils and teachers as conscripts in the innovative campaigns launched by others; the second is the idea of pupils and teachers as puppets, dancing on the strings of other people's visions; and the third is of teachers and pupils as curriculum actors, whose fate it is to act out plots that other people have written. The common ground among these images is clear: it is the right of teachers and students, as partners in the daily enactments of the classroom, to understand what they are doing and why they are doing it, to recognize the areas where they can, together, influence and improve the experience of learning and teaching, and to appreciate, each in their own way, that the goal is to extend the possibility of control over one's own working environment and life chances through deeper professional and personal understanding.

If there is one text that has influenced my thinking it is a passage from Hinton's *Fanshen* (1966). The term 'fanshen' is explained (p. vii):

> Literally, it means "to turn the body" or "to turn over". To China's hundreds of millions of landless and land-poor peasants it meant to stand up, to throw off the landlord-yoke, to gain land, stock, implements and houses. But it meant much more than this. It meant to throw off superstition and study science, to abolish "word blindness" and learn to read, to cease considering women as chattels and establish equality between the sexes. . . . It meant to enter a new world.

The book describes the struggle for change in a Chinese village whose people 'had transformed themselves from passive victims of natural and social forces into active builders of a new world' (p. 609). As the author explains:

> This, as I understood it, was the essence of *fanshen*.
> The more I examined the process of the development of consciousness the more complex it appeared. It worked its leaven on many levels at

once – on the individual, on the community, and on the nation – and at each level of the process followed its own peculiar patterns.

When one broke *fanshen* down to the microcosm, to what happened inside any given individual, it was obvious that no person could break free of the past all at once. The spectrum of man's consciousness could not be refocused in one night no matter how earnestly he might desire such a shift. Change had to come first in one area, then spread to others. It had to dissolve old contradictions only to set up new ones. It had to expand the struggle between the new and the old until the entire personality became involved in painful conflict. No one going through such inner strife exhibited a character that was all of one piece. Habits, superstitions, and prejudices left over from the past marred and undermined efforts to act on the enlightened motives of the present.

Pursuing the agenda

During the 1970s, I was energetically engaged in the then controversial teacher-as-researcher movement. Lawrence Stenhouse and Barry MacDonald had seen curriculum development projects as offering teachers ideas about teaching and learning alongside evidence of how these ideas had been interpreted in the different settings of pilot schools. On the basis of these offerings, teachers were invited to construct their own critical response. 'Using research means doing research', wrote Stenhouse (1979): in other words, a proper response to externally designed curriculum projects is research-based implementation. A parallel argument was used by Illich (1981) in relation to the notion of 'science for people' and 'science by people': he advocated the mediating power of a critical technology that can help practitioners make intelligent use of what so-called experts offer who are distant from the realities of practitioners' everyday living. In the 1980s, the debate about teacher research was intensified and, in 1990, when this book was completed, teacher research was being hailed by some writers (e.g. Lawn, 1989; Carr, 1989a) as the major oppositional and emancipatory force in the face of increasing centralized control.

A project on exploring issues of race in the classroom was designed in the mid-1970s (see Stenhouse *et al.*, 1982) specifically to give teachers a research role, with the small central team of CARE staff acting as co-ordinators and partners in the task of analysing what the effects were, in different settings, of the teaching strategies that teachers were using. The teachers also acted as disseminators, offering detailed analyses of their collective and individual experiences within the project. They organized and led workshops for a variety of audiences and I played the role of project historian. *Pilgrims' Progress* would have been an apt title for the project report: the teachers carried the heavy burden of their own professionalism. Academics and local advisers were not ready, at that time, to listen to teachers and learn from them; other teachers who had paid to attend the workshops were disoriented not to find the usual hierarchy of conference 'names' and were wary of the single-minded commitment of this small band of teacher researchers.

It was during this period that John Elliott and Clem Adelman were developing their impressive Ford Teaching Project that widely legitimized the idea of teachers learning from the detailed study of their own teaching in partnership with university researchers. I went on to explore the potential of different kinds of research partnerships, working with Nick May and a group of primary and middle school teachers on a study of gender issues, and working with Alan Sigsworth on different ways of developing observation partnerships that would allow teachers to see their familiar routines and practices from different angles. I also worked with Charles Hull on ways of helping teachers find out what kind of thinking, and what quality of thinking, was going on in their different subject lessons. In each of these projects, we were interested in the role of university-based outsiders in fostering small-scale, classroom-based research initiatives that would enable teachers to sustain the excitement of professional learning.

Another project grew directly out of my teaching the HCP for a couple of periods a week in a local comprehensive school. This was a key experience for me, as I felt, at first hand, both the weight of convention that innovations were struggling to lift, and the way that we commonly neglect to involve pupils in the process of change. Too often pupils are the victims of change and, faced with unexplained and unjustified disturbances in their routines, they can use their considerable skill in the manipulation of social situations to undermine change. They can thus represent a force for conservatism in the classroom. Charles Hull and I explored these ideas in a project where, again working closely with teachers, we tried out different strategies for helping pupils to make the transition from one way of learning to another. We ran conferences for pupils, helped them to devise their own criteria for judging their progress with the new learning strategies, and reflected back some sense of the importance of their collective achievements alongside their individual performances. Later, I was one of the field workers in Lawrence Stenhouse's and Beverly Labbett's project on academic learning in sixth forms where we interviewed large numbers of students[1] in 24 settings to see how young people pursuing academic courses in the prestigious institution of the British sixth form were treated, and whether they were in fact enjoying the privilege of responsibility that, in our view, should not be preserved for only the relatively small proportion of young people who stay on at school beyond the statutory leaving age.

In 1983, I decided to wrench myself away from CARE. Lawrence Stenhouse had died in the autumn of 1982 and for me that was the end of an era. Despite my unabated respect and love for my old CARE colleagues, Barry MacDonald and John Elliott, I wanted a fresh start. I applied for the Chair of Education at Sheffield University, and in 1984 I took over responsibility for initial teacher training and later set up, with John Gray, a research group committed to looking at the complementarity of qualitative and quantitative studies of change and school effectiveness in education.

At Sheffield I became involved in a study of cooperative group work in secondary schools with Helen Cowie and Karen Dunn and hovered on the edges – an 'on-call' role – of a project developing new teaching and learning strategies in biotechnology. I also witnessed Sheffield's attempt to launch a bold school-development programme, in partnership with two higher education institutions, which was designed to foster and celebrate the idea of schools' ownership of change. Ironically, the celebration of ownership was overtaken, even before its significance could be fully explored, by the imperatives of the national curriculum and its intricate assessment frameworks.

The late 1980s saw strong government intervention at every level of education. New structures for initial and in-service teacher education were marketed on the notion of giving more professional control to teachers, but they seemed, instead, designed both to reduce the influence that universities have on teacher education and to create professional vulnerability as the massive centralized reforms started to roll, like armoured tanks, into the streets of the school system up and down the country.

Now, in 1990, the public image of teaching and the morale of teachers is low and teacher shortages are leading to emergency recruitment strategies which are likely to extend the process of deskilling. The educational climate is profoundly anti-intellectual and there is a lot to be done in helping rebuild public respect for the profession and ensuring that a creative and constructive relationship can continue between universities and schools, with research, research-based teaching and research-based teacher education as its common concerns. This will be my agenda for the next few years.

Note

I have used the word 'pupil' for young people who attend school up to the age of 16; the word 'student' is used for young people post-16 who stay on in the sixth form or who go to a further education or tertiary college.

2 Understanding the Problems of Innovation and Change

> Secondary education has for more than half a century been undergoing a serious crisis which has by no means reached its conclusion. Everybody feels that it cannot remain as it is. . . . Everywhere educationalists and statesmen are aware that the changes which have occurred in the structure of contemporary societies, in their domestic economies as in their foreign affairs, require parallel transformations, no less profound, in the special area of the school system. (Durkheim, 1977, quoted in Brown, 1987, p. 183)

Calls for change have come at us from all sides, some plain and practical, others urgent and impassioned. The need for change has been expressed in terms of the economy and many groups have said that we need a workforce that has the technological skill to compete in the international market. The need for change has been expressed in terms of the state of society:

> In a society disfigured by class exploitation, sexual and racial oppression . . . the only education worth the name is one that forms young people capable of taking part in their own liberation. (Connell *et al.*, 1982, quoted in Giroux, 1983, p. 114)

The need for change has been expressed in terms of the self-concept of young people:

> Our present secondary school system exerts on many pupils a destruction of their dignity, particularly but by no means exclusively [pupils] from the working class. . . . When dignity is damaged, one's deepest experience is of being inferior, unable and powerless. (Hargreaves, 1982, p. 17)

Proposals for change, although issuing from quite different sources have, interestingly, been expressed in remarkably similar terms, and they are about much more than basic skills and the modernization of curriculum content. The DES (1985) has maintained that pupils need more opportunity to learn for themselves, to express their own views, and to develop their ideas through discussion. The Training Agency, through its Technical and Vocational Education Initiative (TVEI), has sought to ensure that the curriculum *for all pupils* will include a technological perspective, but it also urges opportunities for active learning. The Secondary Heads Association has called for teaching styles that will promote autonomy among pupils rather than passive dependence, and that will foster resourcefulness and a sense of interdependence. The Royal Society of Arts, in its Education for Capability Programme, has emphasized the importance of tasks that are real and that support pupils in working cooperatively together. Other voices call for a curriculum that will permit pupils to take more responsibility for their own learning, to appreciate the strength of their own cultural resources, and to participate in evaluating their own learning. These proposals are not, on the surface, greatly in conflict. The agenda for change is pretty clear. We see where we should be going. The problem is getting there and, in the UK, the new Education Reform Act may well make the journey more difficult. Nevertheless, it is timely to reflect on what we have learned from earlier efforts to guide us in moving forward.

Innovation without change

The launching of Sputnik in the 1950s was an event that crystallized, in a publicly comprehensible and therefore convenient form, already mounting concern in the West about the status of knowledge in the school curriculum. There followed, first in the USA and then in other countries, a wave of subject-specific curriculum renewal programmes, with maths and science courses the first targets. Since then, the content of many traditional areas of the secondary curriculum has been updated, and new areas have found a place in the curriculum, e.g. combined humanities, health education, personal and social education, computer studies. Active Tutorial Work has, in some schools, given structure and common purpose to what I remember as the casual encounters of the form period. In short, teachers' experience over the past 10–15 years is of a curriculum that is ever changing. But over the same period, observers and evaluators of the curriculum scene in different educational systems where curriculum reform has been actively pursued offer judgements that are difficult to square with the everyday experience of teachers. For example, a Canadian writes:

> While change in society has become commonplace, the schools remain much as they always were . . . despite huge efforts the educational establishment at all levels has shown a remarkable inability to implement and maintain more effective ways of teaching or to create school settings that are productive and exciting learning environments for schools. (Wideen, 1987, p. 1)

An Italian notes:

Reactive and resistant mechanisms function to preserve school behaviour in a context of innovation and change. (Rosario, 1986, p. 35)

Two Swedish educationists comment:

It can be said that by and large [schools] have not changed fundamentally over some decades. (Tangerud and Wallin, 1986, p. 45)

An American writes:

The most remarkable feature of the educational system is its capacity for continuity and stability in the face of efforts at change. . . . [We are confounded by] the inability of innovations to transform the schools. (House, 1979, pp. 9–10)

And another American, with a more cynical view of change, says this:

When we speak of an innovative school, we mean one that tries one new thing after another without making any of them work. (Runkel, 1984, p. 178)

We are left with a paradoxical impression of stability and yet change, of diversity and yet sameness. We can try to explain this paradox by distinguishing between change that affects the deep structures of schooling, and developments that alter day-to-day practice but not always the way teachers and students think about schooling. We may have learned how to introduce new content and new materials into the curriculum, but it seems that we are not so adept at changing the process of teaching and learning: too often the new content is conveyed in the baggage of traditional pedagogy (see Fullan, 1982, p. 28).

John Goodlad (1984) reported a study of 1000 elementary and high school classrooms in the USA. The study was conducted in the wake of the massive curriculum reform movement of the 1960s and 1970s. He concluded that while individual teachers, as in the UK, may yield impressive results in difficult circumstances, the overall picture was only too familiar. Goodlad (1984, p. 123) observed that:

- the dominant pattern of classroom organisation was still whole class teaching;
- much of the interaction was determined by the need to maintain orderly relationships among twenty to thirty people in a confined space;
- students essentially worked alone within a group setting;
- classes were usually praised for the sum of their individual performances rather than for any collaborative accomplishment;
- the teacher was the main determiner of activities;
- students engaged in a narrow range of classroom activities;
- there was remarkably little evidence of joy in learning, and the emotional tone of the succession of lessons that made up the students' school day was remarkably uniform.

In our efforts at change I think we have generally underestimated the power of the existing culture of the school and classroom to accommodate, absorb or expel innovations that are at odds with the dominant structures and values that hold habit in place. We hear how novel features of innovations are blunted in an effort to fit them into established patterns of practice (Goodlad *et al.*, 1970, p. 72). While some individual schools have managed to transform themselves, there seems little evidence across schools of initiatives surviving that have successfully challenged the existing framework of values and teaching styles. The different observers conclude that schools seem to 'change in appearance and not much in depth' (Tangerud and Wallin, 1986, p. 45), or that recent innovations may only 'rearrange the technical surface' of the classroom (Popkewitz *et al.*, 1982, p. 21), and that what we have are 'simply recycled and repackaged forms of the existing rationality' (Giroux, 1981, p. 150).

Why is it so difficult to achieve fundamental curriculum change in schools? What we are up against, I suggest, is the tenacious conservatism of institutions. Alvin Toffler, in his book *Future Shock* (1970), argued that the prevailing ideology of schooling was established at the time when the idea of mass education became popular and that it is held in place by so many social and political straps that the structure is difficult to dismantle. The organization of knowledge into disciplines, the parcelling out of time, the regimentation, the system of seating, grouping, grading and marking, the image of the teacher – these are all residual features of a powerful bureaucratic model. The tight weave of traditions and routines, combined with the loose coupling of their internal communication systems, can make schools almost as impermeable as a fortress.

But we have to accept, at some level, that schools are properly conservative. We rely on their continuities to ensure 'the duration of character, of intelligent action, and of civilisation' (Watson, 1973, p. 117). We should be comforted by the thought that schools are not easily thrown into disarray by curricular fads and fancies, whimsical novelties and light persuasions. The problem is that they seem almost equally impervious to what we think of as our reasoned, relevant and legitimate proposals for curriculum change.

I want now to look critically at the two main strategies for curriculum change that we have relied on in this country during the last 15 years or so – before legislation came to be used as a strategy for system-wide reform:

- large-scale, centrally funded, national curriculum projects; and
- school-based curriculum development activities.

The curriculum development movement in the UK suffered I think from the technocratic/bureaucratic assumptions out of which it was constructed in the USA. In its pure form, the model was arrogantly simplistic and somewhat neglectful of a school's sense of its own identity. The focus was on the mass-produced curriculum package and its transmission, its installation and its integrity. The ownership of meaning remained with its originators. The logic of the new courses, and the theory of learning that informed and gave them co-herence, was not always made explicit and teachers did not feel, in many cases, intellectually in control. In-service courses designed to prepare teachers to handle the new curricula frequently recruited only one teacher from a school rather than a working group of teachers, and shared meanings were not built up. In the privacy of the teacher's own classroom, it was all too easy for the regularities of past practice to creep back and muzzle the innovation.

At a national level, the problem of understanding change was quickly shunted into the problem of categorizing and measuring change. Success was often related to what could easily be demonstrated – project take-up figures derived from publishers' sales records, for instance, or the number of times a particular project 'label' appeared on school timetables. The quality of teachers' understanding of the new ideas and what they meant for ways of organizing and assessing learning received much less attention.

Another problem was that the curriculum projects were, in the main, concerned with separate bits of the curriculum. There was no coherent framework of principles across projects: at most they were linked by a loose commitment to discovery and inquiry learning methods. The effects were inevitably piecemeal. The curriculum development movement could not, by virtue of its project structure, address itself to the task of holistic curriculum development.

The central curriculum development teams kept their hard-won knowledge of the curriculum process too much to themselves and did not leave a strong legacy of expertise in the construction of new curricula to the school-based teams that succeeded them. They did not work hard enough at finding ways of bringing teachers into the world of curriculum deliberation that they created and inhabited (see Rudduck, 1986a). In particular, they did not do enough to help teachers see that curricula can be designed to embody hypotheses about learning that teachers can test in the particular conditions of their own classrooms.

For all their weaknesses in communication, the departure of the big projects was an intellectual loss. What was distinctive about them was that their central teams had the time to tackle fundamental curriculum issues in ways that are often beyond the scope of school-based teams whose members have a full teaching load. Teaching requires such energy that radical curriculum change – that which confronts issues of power and equality through pedagogy – is unlikely to be achieved without time, without resources, without space to distance one's self from everyday routine, and without opportunities for focused and critical dialogue with people who can offer different perspectives on the task of change. School-based curriculum development sounds good:

> All our liberal reflexes resonate when we consider the idea of schools developing and teaching their own curricula, adapted to the unique constellation of factors which make up each and every school's milieu. (Gordon, 1987, p. 29)

But it is difficult to do it well. School-based curriculum development can, as Gordon notes, ensure local relevance, what Schwab (1970, quoted in Westbury and Wilkof, 1978) describes as a sense of a particular group of pupils, 'of a particular locus in time and space, with smells, shadows, seats and conditions outside the [school] walls which may have much to do with what is achieved inside'. This is the obvious and seductive strength of school-based curriculum development – something that a centrally developed project can never achieve. But intimacy has its own problems. The limits of possibility may be determined by expectations rooted in the familiar past. Ways of thinking may be constrained by routine patterns of perception that support routine patterns of behaviour, and ambitious alternatives may not easily be considered. The price of local relevance may be, given the conditions under which teachers have in the past had to attempt school-based curriculum development, either lack of pedagogic coherence and rigour, or an unwitting conservatism.

To summarize, what we have learned from our efforts at curriculum change since the 1970s is that the task is formidable. We know that curriculum change is not a simple, mechanical process that needs an expert kick to get it going when it stalls (Rosario, 1986, p. 39). We know that the quick fix of the curriculum package is not enough. We know that we have to tackle issues of process and assessment alongside issues of content. We know that we have to plan in terms of the curriculum as a whole. But the main achievement in our learning is that we are beginning to see change not simply as a technical problem but as a cultural problem that requires attention to context and to the creation of shared meaning within working groups. Ironically, just as we arrive at this understanding, the UK government demands that schools set complex new structures in place with a speed that does not permit the deliberative building of shared meaning.

Curriculum change and the problem of building shared meaning

When we talk about creating shared meaning in the working group, which people do we have in mind? The whole staff of a school? The staff of a department? Teachers and advisers? Teachers and governors? Do we think of the pupils? Too often they are our blind spot. If we are to be true to the real principles of curriculum reform – 'pupil-centred learning', a 'negotiated' curriculum, 'transforming the experience of pupils' – then we have to consider the part pupils play in curriculum change. One reason why we fail to root new pedagogies in sustained classroom practice is, I think, because we underestimate the force for conservatism that pupils can represent. They are as much guardians of the present culture as teachers. A 16-year-old school leaver once said: 'You could build it all of marble, but it would still be a bloody school.' Part of our task in attempting fundamental curriculum change is helping pupils to believe that schooling *can* be different.

We also have to find better ways of creating shared meaning and a shared commitment to curriculum change among individuals and working groups of teachers in schools (see Sarason, 1982). Many teachers question, in the face of planned change, why there appears to be so little regard for what they have already accomplished. Change involves the adaptation or abandonment of practices that are familiar and therefore comfortable. If change is seen as a denial of a person's professional past, then his or her investment in a change programme will at most be slender. 'Occupational identity represents the accumulated wisdom of how to handle the job', said Marris (1975, p. 16): change can threaten the basis of one's occupational identity. It is important, therefore, that those who are to be involved in change are helped to see that there is a continuity in experience and in the professional knowledge that experience creates. Moreover, teachers must come to feel that they recognize as significant the problem or situation that is defining the agenda for change, and that they are partners in the planning of change.

If an initiative for change comes from outside the school, then the staff will need to give local meaning to the abstractions of national or regional policy. There must be opportunities for collaborative analysis of the need for change, of the strategies by which change is to be achieved, and of the criteria for judging what progress towards change teachers and their pupils are making. Teachers must feel as individuals and as members of a working group that they own and are in control of the problem of change. Dialogue within working groups is crucial, 'not as a matter of empty courtesy or ritualistic adherence to some vague democratic ethos' (Sarason, 1982, p. 217), but to bring people in on the logics of planned change.

But building shared meaning among members of a school staff (let alone between teachers and their pupils) is easier said than done. There are few institutional conventions that support time spent on exploring the meanings that underpin practice. Staff meetings in secondary education, as well as in higher education, are filled with business, and there is often little time to deal sensitively and constructively with fundamental issues. While we manage to communicate regularly about administrative matters, we do not always make time to explore each other's views of teaching and learning. We measure out our lives, as T.S. Eliot (1958) says, with talk of coffee spoons rather than talk of curriculum. Moreover, as has been noted (Anderson and Snyder, 1982), education is among the last vocations where it is still legitimate to work by yourself in a space that is secure against invaders: the word colleague can refer to a relative stranger on the other side of the wall. Any attempt to create an environment for fundamental change in schools will need to bring about an increase in opportunities for collaborative planning and sharply lengthen the amount of time available for professional discussion (see Joyce *et al.*, 1983, p. 69).

I think we all understand that the irony of effecting substantial curriculum change is that you cannot close the school for a year in order to desocialize the inhabitants, transform the school working spaces so that they look different, and convince pupils and parents – or at least secure a willing suspension of disbelief. Teachers have to maintain their commitment to present structures while planning new approaches; they have to fulfil present expectations while considering strategies for changing those expectations. They will experience, to say the least, a mild schizophrenia. The appropriate virtues for the task of fundamental curriculum change are imagination, patience and immense fortitude.

I have tried to distinguish between change that affects the deep structures of the curriculum and change that affects the surface of the curriculum. I have proposed that we try to see change not as a technical problem but as a cultural problem and that we stop talking *just* about the management of change – a phrase that has dominated educational thinking and writing for a long time – and start talking, instead, about the meaning of change.

PART 2

Challenging Traditional Values and Assumptions

Introduction

School improvement, as Ruth Jonathan (1987, p. 568) reminds us, is not merely a matter of 'rapid response to changing market forces through a trivialised curriculum', but a question of dealing with the deep structures of school organization and the habits and values they embody. The way forward is not to programme pupils 'in a certain direction so that they will behave in set ways' (Aronowitz and Giroux, 1986, p. 9), but to help them towards a reasoned and responsible autonomy. Schools must be committed to the task of helping young people exercise power over their own lives:

> The school does not give people their political ideals or their religious faith but the means to discover both for themselves. Above all it gives them scepticism so that they leave with the ability to doubt rather than the inclination to believe. (Rae, 1973, p. 380)

Would that it were so! The critical thinking that fosters scepticism and independence of mind is too much absent from the curriculum of the comprehensive school. The man who made the statement quoted above was head of an independent school, and one recalls Stenhouse's (1980a) challenge: 'Is the entry into critical thinking to be the privilege of an educated oligarchy? Is it being stifled in the state system?'

The problem is that teachers and pupils often conspire in perpetuating a false security that manifests itself in a reliance on right answers and on a view of the expert as one who knows rather than as one who uses knowledge to refocus doubt. Teachers, prompted by a kindly concern for the young people they teach, often over-simplify the complexities of living and learning; they seek to protect their pupils from uncertainty. Consequently, it is not easy for pupils to escape from what Giroux (1981, p. 81) calls 'the tyranny of imposed meaning'. We must first strip away the layers of unexamined reality that hide behind 'the facts' and help pupils and teachers sever their dependence on the chimera of intellectual certainty. Many teachers in their period of professional training have not acquired the intellectual tools they need in order to view knowledge as problematic. Many pupils find it hard to conceive of questioning adults after years of regarding knowledge as something that lies between the covers of the textbook or that exists in the teacher's mind. In short, the classroom has not generally been an arena for the exercise of critical thinking. There are, of course, exceptions – individual teachers, particular schools – where there is a commitment to help all young people 'use their minds'. But in many schools, teachers continue to regard 'thinking' as the proper aspiration only for older or for more academically able pupils.

In a recent study, Reba Page (1989) offers striking evidence of this. Families sending their children to Southmoor School in the USA were almost exclusively white middle- or upper-class and the pupil body was both academically and socially advantaged. There was almost total commitment to the ideal of an academic curriculum. Within the school there was, however, a small population of academically less successful pupils who nevertheless expressed their support for the school and what it stood for. These pupils followed a 'lower track' curriculum that was still designed to tackle academic content. The main difference between the lower track and the regular track curriculum was the pedagogy. In the regular classes, teachers promoted debate: 'Civil but serious intellectual exchanges were the currency' and students 'were expected to develop critical thinking skills . . . the teachers presented students with complex questions fairly dripping with controversy'. But in lower track classes, the possibility of disagreement was to a large extent avoided by a reliance on 'individual seat work, films, silent reading, and social activities'. The pupils 'were enjoined to think' but they were encouraged, unlike their regular track peers, 'to keep into the teacher's ideas' (p. 209). On those occasions where pupils managed to raise an issue that was on the margins of controversy, 'the disagreements . . . were rather quickly woven back into the on-going flow of talk'. In the lower tracks, debate was seen as a challenge to the authority of the teacher rather than, as in the regular tracks, an intellectual enquiry that pupils and teachers could pursue together. The lower track pupils came to learn 'that they had few legitimate means of expressing academic competence or interest' (p. 218) and that their main contribution to the school was to stay out of the way of its 'main operation of academic pre-eminence'. This study powerfully highlights the dynamic of differentiation that is often documented in relation to schools that have more disadvantaged pupils within their total population.

In this section of the book, the issues raised by Page are explored in different contexts. Chapter 3 is an account of teaching and learning in a number of academic sixth-form settings in the UK. It suggests, however, that there is less commitment to the development of critical thinking in academically oriented groups than Page found in the regular tracks of her high school. The study reveals a considerable gap between the conventional sixth-form rhetoric of fostering independence of thinking and the reality of everyday practice. There is a clear enhancement of social privilege and responsibility but not much evidence, in an examination-dominated environment, of the nurturing of independence of mind. That, it seems, is to be enjoyed only in the promised land of undergraduate life – and even here some students would say that it is pretty elusive!

Chapter 4 argues for the potential of cooperative group work and discussion-based learning to be taken seriously in schools. It recognizes the strength of the traditions and perspectives that group work challenges, and underlines the complexity of the concerns that shape teachers' and pupils' responses. Evidence from a recent study suggests that group work can be used in ways that, albeit unwittingly, reinforce patterns of divisive practice; moreover, in some settings, only its more superficial benefits – as a break from routine or as a quick classroom pick-me-up – are recognized, and its more profound possibilities for helping young people to think for themselves remain largely unrealized.

Innovations that set out to grapple with these issues have, at some level, to be concerned with the transformation of consciousness through which we can begin to think of new cultural possibilities for our schools (see Slaughter, 1989). This is not an easy task, for as Maxine Greene (1985, quoted in Smyth, 1987a, p. 156) has said: '. . . schools seem to resemble natural processes: what happens in them appears to have the sanction of natural law and can no more be questioned or resisted than the law of gravity'. That is the nature of the challenge which innovation must respond to.

3 'A Majority Ruled by Knowledge'?*

We are still two nations (because we produce, through education, a minority served by knowledge) and a majority ruled by knowledge . . . an intellectual, moral and spiritual proletariat, characterised by instrumental competencies rather than autonomous powers. (Stenhouse, 1983b, p. 166)

In schools in the UK, 'the sixth form' has become an institution in its own right. It has traditionally marked the gap between the majority who leave school at 16 and the minority who have stayed on to pursue academic courses of study leading to university entrance or to other 'professional' routes. During periods of high youth unemployment, more young people choose to stay on at school and the narrow academicism of the sixth form is thus gradually modified. The present move in some LEAs towards tertiary reorganization, where all young people opting to stay on in education go to a 'comprehensive college' that offers a full range of 'academic', 'technical' and 'vocational' courses, means an end to the traditional sixth form as we have known it.

Before the moves towards reorganization had gained momentum, we looked at sixth-form teaching in 20 schools. We were interested in seeing whether the cultivation of 'independence of mind' that has long been claimed as the mark of sixth-form teaching and learning was much in evidence in the face of a highly competitive public examination system (the UK's 'A' level system). We wanted to ask why, if teachers have the pedagogic skills and strategies to foster independence of thinking in sixth-form students, they do not extend their aspirations to pupils – the majority – who leave full-time education at the age of 16.

Teachers commonly expect a marked change in the attitude and behaviour of young people when they enter the sixth form. In our conventional parlance,

---

*This chapter is based on passages from a book – a project report – written by Jean Rudduck and David Hopkins (1984).

the change, effected during the span of the summer holiday, is from being 'a pupil' to being 'a student'. In timetabling terms, students generally study fewer subjects at greater depth and have free periods when they do not need to attend classes. Not all students are able to manage the free time well. The problem of organizing one's own time in the face of an agenda of tasks could be seen as reproducing, in the setting of the school, professional or managerial conceptions of time in relation to work; the academic sixth form has, of course, traditionally dealt with students who were expected to take up occupations that ask for a discipline similar to that which the situation demands of them. Such a perception would prompt an analogy between the heavily directed work of the lower school and the character of routine, sub-professional employment.

In the sixth form, the combination of somewhat more flexible timetabling and of work loads that are both longer-term and more variable means that one of the most consistent features of 'independent study' as it is experienced by sixth formers is the responsibility for organizing and for motivating one's own work. The need for organization could be seen as the need for sensible planning. The motivation problem is one of self-discipline – even if you can plan your work rationally, you may not execute your plan. In this respect, independence is less a privilege than an assumption of the burdens of responsibility. In short, one aspect of independent study – self-discipline or self-motivation – constitutes an increase in responsibility more conspicuously than it offers an invitation to freedom. It constitutes a potential 'moral' dimension, an area in which the Protestant work ethic brings rewards; and, consequently, it places teachers in a position to moralize to their students about work habits.

Alongside the idea of independence as responsibility for one's own work, is the idea of independence of mind. This is an ideal for many teachers and many students in the sixth form, but it is not consistently pursued, and in the majority of schools we studied there were considerable differences of perspective and practice. Now, although independence of mind can be treated simply as a matter of originality, in the end it entails confronting the difficult issue of epistemology, for there is no case for independence unless the ideal of freedom of thought can be accepted, and this in turn implies a conviction that knowledge is constructed by thought rather than revealed by authority.

The simple schemata presented overleaf emphasize the differences, as we perceived them, between 'independence as responsibility' and 'independence as freedom of thought'.

While most students acquire a sense of 'independence as responsibility', not all come to experience 'independence as freedom of thought'. The main barrier is the residue of attitudes to authority that pupils have been socialized into during the period of compulsory education and that, as students, they cannot easily shake off.

Kicking the dependence habit is not easy: the problem is, when do you stop believing the teacher? The strongest evidence of students' intellectual dependence on the teacher is their reliance on the notes taken in class. Because notes are seen by so many students as the crutch on which they will depend for the examination, their preference for the security of notes structured or dictated by

---

A: 'Social organization of work'

- Independence as responsibility
- The work ethic
- Organization of task and time
- Independence as a socio-psychological principle

B: 'Social organization of knowledge'

- Independence as freedom of thought
- The play of ideas
- Organization of thinking and mind
- Independence as an epistemological principle

---

the teacher can outweigh their concern for their right as students to make their own notes. When students go beyond what is given in class, the investment of energy is often finely calculated and the motivation is straightforwardly instrumental: the examiner is likely to respond well to the injection of a few touches of authenticity and individuality into the common data provided by the lesson notes and the standard textbook. The point of reading is, for many students, limited to the confirmation of an argument, not to its development. Of course, there are students who seek more and who are restless with styles of teaching that do not help them to take their own thinking seriously, but on the whole the images are of a rhetoric of independence belied by instructional teaching and a narrow view of knowledge.

Good sixth-form teaching introduces students to the ways of thinking within their discipline, so that they are not merely 'doing history' but 'being historians'. The tragedy is that the entitlement to 'use your mind' is so rarely honoured.

Some evidence from the interviews

The authority of the teacher and the growth of intellectual independence

> . . . his notes are very full anyway and those books we look in are a spread out of his notes, and his notes are a spread out of the books – there's not much more . . . to be found.

Where, in class, the teacher summarizes the basic textbook, and the student reads no books other than the basic textbook, then there is little possibility of divergence of interpretation. This incestuous cycle reinforces the authority of the teacher and it is only the stronger students, who are learning to tread the waters of independence, who readily accept what good sixth-form teaching can reveal – both the limitations of the teacher's knowledge and the provisionality of knowledge itself.

For some students, dependence on what the teacher offers is enforced by circumstance as well as by habit: 'Extra information is hard to come by really' and so the student feels confined to the territory and contours of the teacher's mind. At the same time, students are ambivalent about the implications of such confinement: a student of German criticizes the tone in which the teacher sets a task – 'I want half a page.' Another student talks about English lessons where the sixth-form teacher 'asks a lot of questions' on each poem, play or novel, and the students 'go through it page by page' with the teacher 'pointing out the important lines and the significance of such and such'. The students become more uneasy when the teacher merely reads the text aloud in the lesson: 'He'll read out of the book, mumble, mumble, mumble, and it is all you can do to keep awake . . . and you can see others making paper aeroplanes – a sixth former making paper aeroplanes! You just can't read a whole section out of a book like that!.' But the students have no strategy for modifying such teaching behaviours.

It is not easy to develop confidence in one's powers after a long and unbroken period of socialization towards dependence on the teacher, and the spectre of the examination inevitably forces students back on to accepting the teacher's questions rather than their own as guides to the proper routes of enquiry, and the teacher's statements as a proper representation of meaning. Indeed, as one student points out, independence at sixth-form level is probably not about ideas so much as self-discipline: 'Well, it is about independent effort. . . . I think you get a lot of help . . . all that is left up to you is actually to do the studying.' Another student, using a strikingly persuasive image, puts it like this: in the sixth form you are 'just let loose on a long lead, really'.

Of course, there is always another stage beyond the present which promises greater independence and more intellectual adventuring. It can be the university:

> . . . at that level it's important that you don't take everything [i.e. what the lecturer says] for granted, but at this stage [i.e. sixth form] I don't think you should take everything for granted . . . but certainly there is a lot more of that here . . . and I wouldn't disagree with it at the moment.

For many students, the teacher is an authority and they are in no position to question the teacher's claim to authority because the pedagogy does not encourage them to seek evidence that might demonstrate the complexity of competing claims to knowledge. Of course, a 'good' teacher is likely to encompass this in his or her teaching, revealing the structure of alternatives that lie behind a synthesis, and justifying the nature of the synthesis, but there are many students for whom knowledge is what the teacher knows:

> The teacher is a doctor, you see, [a doctor of philosophy] and he knows everything.

. . . and if you find something in a book which doesn't say what the teacher tells you, then on the whole you tend to think . . . that the teacher is right and that the book's wrong – which is bad in a way, but you do it.

Some students manage to break away – perhaps because their teachers help them – and enjoy a fledgeling independence of thought. They are learning to accept that their teacher is no longer claiming certainty and cannot therefore be relied on to go on holding out an intellectual safety net for them. They see that students must begin to take responsibility for their own intellectual performances:

In the sixth form, even if what they say is "right", you have got to stand back from what they say and ask: "Are they totally right about that?" and not just write it down as they say it and not think about it.

You've always got to be having it in your head, the word "bias". I mean, whatever information you are given, whether you read it or you are told, I have often the tendency to take that as fact. . . . I mean the whole idea of A level, not necessarily A level, the whole idea of higher education is to question it for yourself and therefore get more out of it for yourself.

These students are beginning to appreciate the play of their own minds; they see that reproducing the idea picked up from the book or the teacher 'is not nearly as much fun as developing your own [ideas] and trying them out'.

One stage in the approach towards independence of thinking is, then, the student's awareness of the limitations of the teacher's knowledge – and the teacher's readiness to acknowledge his or her limitations:

[Lower down in the school] you thought that the teachers knew every-thing. You asked them something and they'd give you the answer. In the sixth form you are not sure about something and you ask your teacher and they'll probably tell you they don't know . . . and it seems a bit strange.

Students who reflect on teachers in this way tend to be courteous rather than cynical about their emergence as real mortals and come to welcome the oppor-tunity to work things out in partnership, with the teacher offering leadership in procedures and ways of learning:

The teachers seem more like students, you know, in the sixth form. He says: "Well, I can't do this" and you show him how to do it and the other way round. We help each other, and the teacher seems to fit in that relationship. I mean we realise if it wasn't for the teacher we wouldn't get anywhere but the relationship is more friendly.

Such a relationship presupposes a confident teacher and not all teachers are prepared to acknowledge weaknesses in their command of their subject – but disguises are easy to penetrate: 'You ask and they say, "I think it is better you don't know that" – which is another way of saying, "I don't know that".'

Instruction and discussion

One mark of professional confidence is the readiness of the teacher to provide opportunities for students to learn through discussion, for it is through discussion that students can explore ideas, begin to challenge unwarranted assumptions and bias, and examine alternatives. Through attempts to express meanings in their own words, students can gain some sense of possession over ideas instead of merely learning the versions that the teacher offers. The transition from instruction to discussion is not easy for student or teacher. If teachers are seen to 'give way' when their opinion is challenged by a student, students feel disconcerted at first, but they may come in time 'to take the evidence a bit more on our own shoulders'. All students seem to appreciate the opportunity for discussion, although some remain suspicious lest the authority of the teacher will ultimately come in to destroy the fragile web of ideas that they are beginning to create, as in lessons where teachers listen to the students talking 'and then say what *they* think'. Alternatively, teachers may take offence if their own ideas, expressed during the discussion, are treated with too little respect and the student then receives a 'How dare you say such a thing' glance! So, in discussion, students are learning to make social judgements about the degrees of freedom individual teachers will tolerate, as well as attending to the intellectual demands of the situation.

Students can also be afraid, in discussion, of exposing their own ignorance or their failure to grasp the structure of the argument and to judge what counts as a relevant contribution. They need help, it seems, in seeing that discussion is an appropriate medium for exploring what people do not understand, and for taking risks with ideas. Apparently, even the more nervous and recessive students would prefer to contribute more to discussion rather than abandon the opportunity. Anxiety can be particularly acute in groups where the perceived range of ability is wide. Instructional teaching does not publicly expose differences of understanding within the student group; the essay is where individual strengths and weaknesses show themselves, and the essay is subject, usually, only to a private viewing by the teacher. So, if you are in 'a high-caste, high-powered set', you are likely to 'just shut up, stay in the background, and if you don't understand it, keep your mouth shut!'

When it comes to noting down – for reflection, or, more likely for revision – points that are made in the discussion, students will selectively write down what their peers say, but more often dependence on the teacher, which always seems to be waiting in the wings, will take over:

> I always put Mr X's ideas down. If he says to us: "I think this" I always put that down because his ideas are so much more, I suppose, complex than mine are. He knows a lot more about it so I make sure that I get down what he says because they're the ones you can rely on more than the rest of the class.

Attitudes and information offered instructionally are, except in the circumstance of some discussion sessions, invariably accepted on the basis of the authority of the teacher's position and training, or the teacher's familiarity with the examination system. It is not surprising, therefore, that students have difficulty, in some subjects, in dealing with the claims to truth made by different 'experts' through the words of their books. If a league table of credibility through status is not available, then students have to face the task of establishing intellectual credibility through the examination of evidence in relation to argument. The criteria for judgement are not easy to define, and students are often unsure whether they are expected merely to line up the different theses, decide and justify the decision as to which is the most credible, or use the different positions (or procedures) to help them formulate a personal view. The uncertainties are abundant:

> I mean, there are two people there who supposedly have been paid an awful lot of money for writing books on it, and they have two entirely different opinions – I mean, what am I supposed to think?

> It is very important to get a lot of books to see what economic historians think, because there is an awful lot of difference and it is rather annoying really. You get one book and you find one thing and then you open another and find somebody else arguing a completely different thing and, of course, you have got to put that in your essay. It is a bit of a fiddly subject.

> Every now and again you get two ideas and each of them have points backing them up and then it starts getting difficult. . . . I usually try to actually make a choice out of the two in history because I end up getting in a muddle if I try and work from sort of two points.

Entwistle (1981) discusses these issues. Summarizing Perry (1970), he suggests how students move from dualistic reasoning – 'believing that there would always be "right" and "wrong" answers to any question' – to contextual relativistic reasoning – 'in which the partial validity of contrasting interpretations of reality was accepted' (p. 116). The problem was certainly much in evidence in our interviews with students.

The teacher's perspective

Many teachers interviewed did not see themselves as facilitators or guides on the students' road to intellectual maturity, but rather as providers of knowledge. Some teachers doubted the capacity, or perhaps even the entitlement, of young people to begin to think for themselves:

> Let's take independence of thought first. I don't expect a great deal of that in the lower [i.e. first year] sixth. I don't expect it in the average candidate in the upper sixth. I expect it from the people who will go on to read their subject at university . . . and some of them develop this to a surprising degree . . . but that doesn't happen to the majority of candidates . . . so that's independent thought!

Expectations are, of course, a powerful determiner of behaviours: if teachers don't expect young people to be capable of thinking for themselves, they will not, in their teaching, create opportunities for them to do so, and young people will, as a result, not develop the capacity for thinking for themselves. Expectations thus become a self-fulfilling prophecy.

On the whole, it seemed that many sixth-form teachers saw their contract with students in terms of ensuring the achievement of good examination grades. Many seemed to protect themselves from facing the fact that teaching for intellectual growth and teaching for examination passes may not be the same. There are more than a few teachers who have succumbed to the tyranny of examinations and who feel that their individual efforts to change their students' expectations are unlikely to succeed. As one sixth-form teacher said, some years back (Fox, 1979, p. 7):

> I think my greatest annual moment of depression is the arrival of a new sixth form fresh from their O level triumph. Sir, Sir, our mouths are open: shovel in The Truth and we'll regurgitate it in the A level. The external examinations, I feel, can trap a teacher and a class mercilessly. If I could, I would ask the sixth form to determine its own course to a very great extent; groups or individuals would make contracts with the teacher to tackle pieces of work, devised in consultation with the teacher – not too closely preplanned to allow room for expansion and alteration as the directions of the group are discovered. The teacher is not an authority figure – but a human centre of information and assistance.

Rarely when interviewed did teachers seriously contest the constraints that examinations impose, and few of those who did so felt that they were in a position to take action. Take history, for instance. From the interviews with history teachers – and it could well apply to teachers of other subjects – we identified four ways in which examinations inhibit the development of an appreciation of, and competence in, the historical method. First, they determine the content to be studied, thereby not allowing an individual's interest to range freely. Secondly, by the nature of the questions they pose, they direct emphasis away from primary sources, which are the foundation of the historian's work, to historical commentaries. Thirdly, they trivialize the nature of historical enquiry by promoting the use of an historical statement (the 30- to 45-minute examination question) in which it is impossible to exercise the full range of the historian's skills. Fourthly, examinations encourage teachers to emphasize techniques for passing examinations, rather than providing training in, and exposure to, the historical method.

In concluding, we return to pedagogy. Whatever is presented in the classroom that is both authoritative and is established 'independently of scholarly warrant' cannot be knowledge; it is faith (Stenhouse, 1983c, p. 181). It is not knowledge, says Stenhouse (perhaps over-confident in the integrity of his university colleagues), 'in the sense in which we in universities deal with it or are equipped to deal with it. Our knowledge is questionable and verifiable and differentially secure.' And, he continues, our students must understand that this is so. Sixth-form teachers tend to justify many of their approaches in terms of preparing students for higher education – but why note-taking and not the nature of knowledge? Teachers cannot vouchsafe truth by virtue of authoritative teaching at any level: teachers of secondary school students are not miraculously free of the error which university teachers are pledged to admit to.

Students are not on the whole – at least in scholastic matters – as well qualified as the teacher and so their way of validating what is offered by the teacher, or by the textbook that the teacher endorses, must be through other sources of knowledge. This is what Stenhouse meant when he talked about the 'student's capacity to appeal against the teacher to the library'. That is not a subversive statement, merely a statement that acknowledges the pedagogical implications of allowing students at sixth-form level to grasp something of the provisional nature of knowledge and the need for critical scrutiny of the evidence that supports claims to truth. It is interesting that a student quoted above asked 'When do you stop believing the teacher?' and not 'Why?' Schools, assuming, it seems, a convenient extension of Piaget's stages of readiness, have decided that the sixth form is the occasion when the first of the seven veils that have successfully hidden the power of knowledge from the innocent eyes of younger pupils can be dropped.

Note

The project was directed by Lawrence Stenhouse and co-ordinated by Beverley Labbett. It was designed as a multi-site case study programme and it involved teachers, students and librarians in 20 schools (14 comprehensive schools, 3 public boarding schools and 3 independent day schools), 2 sixth form colleges, 1 college of further education and 1 tertiary college. The selection took account of the need to have access to different environmental and social settings and different levels of library provision. The main method of data gathering was the interview, and interviews were conducted with 200 sixth-form students, 200 sixth-form teachers, 50 library staff and 60 head teachers, principals or teachers with special responsibility for the sixth form (see Rudduck and Hopkins, 1984).

4 Cooperative Group Work: Democracy or Divisiveness?

Many teachers . . . expect pupils miraculously to be able to participate fluently and naturally, and to be critical and discerning in their intellectual and social behaviour when they leave the fifth and sixth year – without having been offered any genuine appreciation or encouragement to do so in the previous ten years of their school lives. (Fielding, 1973, quoted in Bridges, 1979, p. 128)

'Teaching and learning through cooperative group work' – it sounds a pretty innocuous and mild-mannered approach that most people in our society would respond to with positive regard. But in fact, despite the well-argued potential of cooperative group work to achieve the capacities mentioned by Fielding, most schools have not brought it into the centre of their curriculum policies, and most teachers have not taken it seriously. Why is this so?

In a recent study (see Cowie and Rudduck, 1988a), we interviewed secondary school teachers in the region about group work and we placed them in four categories: 'non-users', 'occasional users', 'divisive users' and 'committed users'. Non-users tended to agree that group work was probably 'a good thing', but they none the less offered all kinds of reasons for not employing it. At some level, the reasons are all real because they reflect pressures on teachers that derive from conventional constructs of what 'a subject' is, what 'teaching' is, what 'being a teacher' is, what 'learning' is and what 'pupils' are like:

What we are trying to achieve in science is the accumulation of facts.

In modern languages the teacher's got to be monitoring everything that goes on.

Art is about individual expression.

Group work? Colleagues might think the lesson is getting out of hand.

Unless you stand over them the kids in this school won't work.

They're quite happy to sit there like little jugs and let you pour it in.

You can't have cooperation at A level.

You see, you've got kids who say, "Mr Jones makes us work. We do real work in his lessons. We're writing it all down."

Non-users also tended to find constraints in rooms, furniture and class size:

The rooms that we have by and large don't lend themselves to group work.

We've got 30 odd in the class for a session that's only 35 minutes. It's rather difficult to do anything other than the traditional style.

There were also, of course, anxieties about personal competence and style, and uncertainties relating to the organization and assessment of group work. Insecurity can easily lead to a protective rejection of what is novel. As one teacher said: 'I think because we're not very familiar with it we may totally disagree with it.' But underlying some of the other explanations offered by teachers for not using group work as a major learning strategy there may be deeper concerns, for group work challenges many of the conventions that provide a platform of personal and professional security.

As Hargreaves (1988) has said, teachers admit to feeling vulnerable and uncomfortable if they move outside tried and tested 'control-centred' teaching strategies where the whole class is treated as a collective pupil (see McNeil, 1987). Cuban (1987, p. 26) offers a sympathetic comment on such strategies, however, explaining their persistence in terms of the idea of 'situationally controlled choice':

Teacher-centred instruction has been a creative response by teachers [to enable them] to cope with work place conditions, conflicting expectations, and structural arrangements over which they had little influence.

To change, as Hargreaves says, we need to support teachers in accepting less 'control-centred educational purposes'. Meanwhile, faced with the herd-like character of large classes, teachers may well continue with the teaching style that fits the particular circumstances of the situation as it is and the particular skills that they have been trained to use.

This teacher-centred style has, of course, been reinforced by a view of school-knowledge as being about the accumulation of certainties. Bruner (1986, p. 123) says that group work, with its valuing of discussion-based learning,

. . . runs counter to traditions of pedagogy that derive from another time, another interpretation of culture, another conception of authority – one that looked at the process of education as a transmission of knowledge and values by those who knew to those who knew less and knew it less expertly.

A powerful perspective holds that instructional teaching is associated with academic success and that academic success is manifest in public examination results:

> I think that because society tends to expect qualifications, and because society expects it, that's what the school gives, and because the school gives it, we [the teachers] have to conform, and because we have to conform, there's no group work. (quoted in Cowie and Rudduck, 1988, p. 15)

Inglis (1989, p. 128) sees in domestic life a similar pattern of individual action being pressed into conformity:

> The new authoritarianism of Britain expresses . . . highly individualised relations of consumption . . . people sit in the living rooms and their spectacular arena is the television screen. Its instrument of organisation is mass consumption seen as an aggregate of countless individual consumer choices.

This image would, I think, endorse the need to help young people experience alternatives to the passive, individualized consumption that has also – without the opportunity to change channel – characterized the more formal and traditional aspects of our teaching styles.

We also talked with teachers whom we classified as 'occasional users'. These teachers regarded group work as a form of refuge. They said things like 'When you're out there at the front all the time, a bit of group work takes the pressure off you.' Connell *et al.* (1982, pp. 102–103) offer a similar picture of the pressures that teachers are trying to take respite from when they write about the 'big strain' of 'constant psychological and physical confrontation with kids'. Teachers see group work as a kind of interlude:

> They're mostly double lessons. It's nice to have a change for a few minutes. Group work allows the kids to relax a bit. I'm all for variety and not just the same old medicine day after day, you know.

And science teachers have said: 'We mostly do group work because there's not enough equipment to go round.' While group work, used in such ways, may increase motivation in the short term, it is clearly not offering pupils any profound social or intellectual challenge (see Cowie and Rudduck, 1988a, p. 52). Indeed, this is a far cry from a perception of discussion-based learning as a way of understanding the nature of personal prejudice, or offering a grounding in the principles of democracy – or pursuing truth. As Popper says (1963, quoted in Bridges, 1979, p. 50):

> Truth is not manifest, and it is not easy to come by. The search for truth demands at least imagination, trial and error, [and] the gradual discovery of our prejudices by way of imagination, trial and error, *and critical discussion.* [emphasis added]

Our 'divisive users' were the most complex. These were teachers who used group work with some pupils but not with others. The differentiation was usually to do with ability. Some divisive users used group work only with their low-attaining pupils for they saw it as a soft – but reasonably motivating – option, and essentially as about personal and social (rather than intellectual) development.

> The group work I do is either in the lower years or with the special needs children.

> I've done it because it's been necessary with the very low-ability children . . . it's not terribly exciting a way out . . . [but] . . . they're enjoying it and they like doing it.

> This is the best way to keep them working because after all . . . their concentration is not good and as long as their friend isn't a real idler it's as well to have them together. (quoted in Cowie and Rudduck, 1988a, p. 52)

Given the combined strengths of both the academic tradition and the teacher-centred tradition in schools, it is perhaps not surprising that group work tends often to be seen as a means of support for lower-attaining pupils. A common fear among teachers is that group work is too casual to foster 'real' learning and that it is not appropriate therefore for 'real' learners:

> I feel that maybe I'm not getting on with it. . . . A bit relaxed, you know, or "laid back" as they say, and there's not quite the grafting that we should be doing.

Teachers who have been used to working with streamed classes of academically higher-attaining pupils and who are skilled in, and satisfied with, formal patterns of teaching can have tremendous difficulty in knowing how to engage the attention of other groups of pupils:

> I can relate a lot better to kids who are like my own, do you know what I mean? Sometimes I feel that I can't get through to the others. I mean, I do the best I can but I can't sometimes get on their wavelength. They'd be better off really doing something practical. (quoted in Cowie and Rudduck, 1988b, p. 16)

Teachers are honest in acknowledging the problems that they have and we begin to understand the structure of concerns that underlie the commonly held view of group work as a form of benevolent but low-status support for the under-privileged.

As Blackmore (1990, p. 178) points out, in Australia, as in the UK, the most successful form of 'vocational' education, in the sense of training for an occupation,

> . . . has been through the "competitive academic curriculum" which has selected and trained the "academically bright" for the professions since

the 19th century. In particular, the hegemony of the academic curriculum has led to the devaluing of alternative . . . curricula.

Discussion-based group work is interesting because it functions, as we saw above, as an instrument of social sorting and selection (ibid.). Those teachers who perceive it as not endorsing academic ends will relegate it to the realm of personal and social education, while those teachers who see the capacity for discussion as a mark of academic privilege will preserve it for their 'academic high-fliers'. A capacity to handle 'serious' discussion (see Page's study summarized in the Introduction to this section) is easily seen as synonymous with a capacity for 'independent thinking' and, as Powell *et al.* (1985) have pointed out in their work with American high schools, most people regard thinking as the 'preserve of smart kids'. They add:

> The schools have done a masterly job at selling the importance of high school attendance, but have failed in the attempt to sell to most students the value of working hard to learn to use one's mind . . . there is little agreement in society or among high school educators that teaching students to use their minds fully is either needed by most youngsters or possible for them. (p. 317)

The absence of evidence of students' capacity to use their minds is not an excuse for not trying to develop that capacity; we must acknowledge that it is we who have constructed that incapacity. Many 'average' students do not learn – and we allow them not to learn: 'Avoidance can be wrapped in brightly packaged illusions. Behind impressive course titles lie the realities of very different classroom treaties' (Powell *et al.*, 1985, p. 310).

The capacity to use one's mind is a precondition of intellectual autonomy and responsible judgement. A major claim of advocates of group work (including our 'committed users'; see Cowie and Rudduck, 1988a) is that it can foster such capacities: instead of pupils and students receiving at second hand the judgements of others, it offers opportunities for active engagement with issues and problems and first-hand experience of thinking things out in dialogue with others. Bridges (1979) offers strong political justification for all young people having opportunities to experience group work in schools. He sees it as fostering capacities that 'lie at the heart of democratic community', capacities that other 'pedagogic procedures like the lecture or other forms of authoritative instruction or individual study' could not be expected to generate (p. 130). In particular, group work requires participants to hear and to take into account different perspectives and it is this capacity, he argues, that is fundamental to the conduct of democracy:

> In the individual pursuit of knowledge or understanding we are locked in the subjectivity of a single perception. . . . Discussion (which is a major component of group work), however, is an activity whose character it is to set alongside one perception of the matter under discussion the several perceptions of other participants. It offers in other words a potential challenge to a perception of the world which is inevitably circumscribed

by the prejudices and imagination of the individual mind, permitting not objectivity perhaps but at least alternative or inter-subjectivity. More simply, discussion enriches or challenges our own view of things with those of others – and this, arguably, is its important contribution to the development of knowledge or understanding. (Bridges, 1979, p. 50).

Wood (1988) suggests that training in these capacities can begin quite early. He argues that children as young as six or seven can be capable of reasoning rationally: 'They can also, in some situations, transcend their own immediate perspective to appreciate what the world looks like from another point of view' (p. 132). The problem is, he says, that adults are so used to taking responsibility for making sense of what young people say that when opportunities are formally provided in school for young people to express and explore meanings, the problems they have in communicating can be interpreted as incompetence or inability, when in fact the problems may be largely due to unreadiness – and it is our own adult behaviours that have contributed to the development of that unreadiness.

We are dealing here with two issues: the need for young people to have opportunities within formal education to take responsibility for expressing themselves in ways that make sense, and the need to provide young people with opportunities to explore other people's perspectives in relation to their own. These two capacities, I suggest, are important components of the 'power of argument', and the power of argument is itself an important feature of the democratic process. The opportunity and capacity to participate fully in the democratic process are, according to Gottlieb (1979, p. 437), not equally available to all young people:

> The ability to argue is itself a power unequally distributed in this society. This observation can be generalised to include the numerous ways in which people of different races, sexes and economic classes are socialised to take unequal roles in a dialogue. (quoted in Groundwater Smith, 1989, p. 43)

In short, the interplay of values and discourses that surrounds the development of group work is more complex than many might at first imagine.

For instance, cooperative group work is, as Gottlieb hints, an arena for confronting issues of gender and class in relation to educational opportunity. The gender issue has also been picked up by Pratt (1987, p. 153), who suggests that the 'individualistic approach, typical both of the traditional and of the technically-oriented curriculum, reflects and exacerbates a masculine model of schooling which discounts the more feminine qualities' – among which are included a concern with process and a commitment to cooperation, each of which could help with the desirable task of deconstructing traditional masculine and feminine images of schooling. And Connell *et al.* (1982) argue that the 'practices of competition' in secondary schools reinforce a particular set of class-linked values that tend to disenfranchise the working-class pupil who is often more familiar with 'practices of cooperative coping'. For these pupils, competition 'is always divisive, always opposed to the sense of common fate and the need for collective response'.

A shift towards group work, if taken seriously, would imply some fundamental rethinking. At one level, 'You have to learn to value the opinions of the students and allow them to take responsibility for what they're doing.' It involves a struggle for the right to determine meaning and opens up the possibility of a different balance of power in the classroom. The capacity for collective response is basic to the self-organization of oppressed or exploited groups and, recognizing this, we can begin to see the nature of the threat that group work presents to traditional structures of schooling. Cooperative group work, handled well and taken seriously, goes some way towards what Aronowitz and Giroux (1986, pp. 36–7) call for; there is an urgent need, they say, to utilize a pedagogy 'that treats students as critical agents, problematizes knowledge, utilises dialogue, and makes knowledge meaningful, critical and ultimately emancipatory'. These are powerful undercurrents for mainstream education to cope with.

However, the threat that discussion-based group work offers is, in practice, relatively contained – and probably likely to remain so, despite recent well-publicized efforts on the part of various agencies, including industry, to extend its use. I suspect that the various initiatives that feature 'group work' will serve to reinforce rather than challenge established values. Despite the current rhetoric of an 'entitlement' curriculum, certain curriculum 'goodies' will continue to be given to those whom the system has disadvantaged, but in ways that underline aspects of their difference. As Hartley (1986) has pointed out, the soft language of cooperation and negotiation tends to be associated with what might be called 'compensatory provision' for certain defined groups of pupils and to be expressed in programmes that focus on social and personal development rather than on thinking and on training in democratic procedures.

Sultana (1989, pp. 287–309) also offers a cautionary tale. He describes a transition (i.e. school-to-work) programme in three secondary schools in New Zealand. It is in such programmes that group work finds a place. But the pupils channelled into the programme were seen by their peers as the 'rejects'. A clear message that the programme itself gave pupils, according to Sultana, was that young people failed to get jobs because they lacked the appropriate personal qualities, not just skills: it was not the structure of the economy that was at fault but the young people themselves. Hence the focus on personal development, the 'editing of the self to match the profile of a perfect prospective employee'. The main agenda was that pupils 'had to somehow change the way they acted, spoke, dressed and thought even – for the tantalising promise of a job' (p. 294). Compliance 'was encouraged overtly' (p. 295): the changes in the way pupils thought was not a move towards greater independence of mind; indeed, the programme seemed to disqualify pupils' from bodies of abstract knowledge from which they could draw interpretations of their life experience' (p. 294). Preparation for work was about the moulding of 'correct' behaviour and attitudes. Such programmes, says Sultana (drawing on the work of Carnoy and Levin, 1985), reflect the 'industrial impulse', rather than the 'democratic impulse'.

To the extent that cooperative group work is strongly associated with such courses and not with others, it is unlikely to meet the profoundly serious aspirations that Bridges and others claim for it. Cooperative group work, despite the flurry of support, will probably still be struggling, in the 1990s, to find its real identity and realize its true potential. David Hargreaves saw the problems in 1980. They have not diminished:

> It is . . . one of the major tasks of education to promote in the learner a commitment to the rights of man. I contend that our present attempts to do so fail precisely because our excessive individualism denies to the pupil those essentially collective experiences which are the necessary medium of such learning. We tend to see collective experiences merely as means of giving students a range of social skills, the capacities to "get along" with other people. This is the social dimension of the cult of individualism – the cult of "chumminess". We become blind to the fact that collective experiences in school are embryonic experiences of social solidarity; and because such experiences will sometimes threaten the rights of individuals, they are experiences in learning to recognize and to respect the rights of individuals. This is Durkheim's paradox: it is only by means of a thoroughly collective experience that a commitment to individual dignity can be learned. The commitment to the rights and dignity of man cannot be taught as a purely intellectual or cognitive experience; it must be apprehended through social experiences.
>
> In our fears of the collective and corporate we may, I suspect, be denying to our pupils [some] essential educational opportunities. (p. 197)

PART 3

Pupil Involvement and Understanding

Introduction

'The first claim on the school is that of pupils for whose welfare the school exists', wrote Lawrence Stenhouse in the mid-1970s (reprinted 1983a, p. 153), and he went on to suggest that instead of emphasizing the responsibilities that pupils should recognize and accept in relation to school and schoolwork, we should also think about the demands that pupils might reasonably make of the school. For instance:

Pupils have a right to demand that the school shall treat them impartially and with respect as persons.

Pupils have a right to demand that the school's aims and purposes shall be communicated to them openly and discussed with them as the need arises.

Pupils have a right to demand that the procedures and organisational arrangements of the school should be capable of rational justification and the grounds of them should be available to them. (see Stenhouse, 1983a, pp. 153–5, for the full manifesto)

The Schools Council's Working Party on the Whole Curriculum, for whom Stenhouse originally drafted this statement in 1975, thought the premise too controversial to publish. Now, in 1990, reactions would be very different. We are much more sensitive to young people's rights, although our practices may be struggling to keep pace with our principles.

In this section, the focus is mainly on the second of the three proposals quoted above – that the logic of the school's aims and purposes should be clear to pupils – but I am mainly interpreting it at the level of the teacher and his or her work in the classroom.

The regularities of schooling unfold themselves day by day for pupils and it is rare for them to have access, as of right, to the curriculum plan that structures a particular course of study. The effect is that many young people come to accept the inevitability of classroom events and do not much question their appropriateness. Or they may simply switch off – a reaction that is also consonant with a view of what happens as being non-negotiable. Indeed, as Chapter 7 suggests, when pupils *are* taken inside the walls of the teacher's mind and given access to the logic that sequences their learning tasks, they are not much bothered to exercise their right to know and to understand.

Chapter 5 focuses on what happens to pupils in a situation of planned change where the world is suddenly destabilized. Deliberation may have continued for some time among the teachers who are involved in the innovation, but for pupils, change tends to be experienced as an unexpected and often unwelcome *fait accompli* rather than as a process whose beginnings and justifications they might expect to be party to. Perhaps more of us in education should share Raymond Williams's 'passionate concern that people who might otherwise find themselves victims of history should be able instead to understand their own circumstances' (Hare, 1989). Chapter 6 is a response to Chapter 5: it records an attempt by a teacher, working alongside university colleagues, to provide an event that might ease the transition from one style of learning to another. The aspiration that lies behind the three chapters in this section is plainly put by Taylor (quoted in Silberman, 1970, p. 402):

> The curriculum, whatever it is, must start with the intention of creating a situation in which the student can honestly commit him [or her] self to what he [or she] is asked to do.

My argument in these chapters assumes that it is enough, for the moment, to find ways of opening up to pupils the school's purposes as expressed in the daily enactments of particular courses of study. But there is, of course, another agenda – about where and in what ways pupils can influence the directions in which their teachers want to take them.

Meighan, in his book *Flexi-schooling* (1989, pp. 36–8), distinguishes between a 'consultative curriculum', a 'negotiated curriculum' and a 'democratic curriculum'. A consultative curriculum, he says, is based on an imposed programme, but regular opportunities for learners to be consulted are built in. Feedback is reflected upon by the teacher and modifications may be proposed. In the negotiated curriculum, 'the degree of power sharing increases': what emerges 'is an agreed contract . . . as to the nature of the course of study to be undertaken'. The negotiation 'constitutes an attempt to link the concerns and consciousness of the learners with the world of systematic knowledge and learning'. Finally, there is the democratic curriculum, 'where a group of learners write, implement and review their own curriculum, starting out with a blank piece of paper'. The learners 'take on the roles of researchers and explorers and the teachers take on the roles of facilitators and fixers'.

The recent imposition of a national framework for the curriculum in the UK, together with highly specific attainment targets, is, I suspect, unlikely to allow teachers to give much time to beginning to work seriously on such an agenda, but there will undoubtedly be schools where teachers already have such a commitment and they are likely to regard pupil involvement and understanding as an important priority for the 1990s.

5 Introducing Innovation to Pupils*

Schools and classrooms are likely to be in a constant state of development. Development rests on small change events, none of which is threatening in itself to the whole structure; on the contrary, each event, though it acts as a minute impulse for change, confirms the known past. Innovation is different: it is conscious, planned, and involves some fundamental breaks with the known past (see Hull and Rudduck, 1981). In referring to 'innovation', I have in mind something that, if realized, would require of those involved a substantial shift from the pattern of their present practices.

In the last 10 years or so, we have made considerable progress in constructing a map that records our understanding of the process of innovation in schools. But there is one area of this map that has not been explored at all systematically. The area I am talking about is the area of pupils and innovation, including how pupils experience change and their power in relation to the progress of an innovation in schools and classrooms.

Why is it that we have given so little attention to these issues in our attempts to study and understand the process of change in schools? Bruce Joyce talks about the problems of incorporation that innovations present to teachers. In particular, he emphasizes the difficulty of integrating new skills or new perspectives into a pattern of behaviour that is already well established and complex in its interrelationships. He points to the difficulties teachers have in operating new skills or new perspectives in situations that have become associated with the old skills and the old perspectives: habits are easy, comfortable and anxiety-free. Joyce mentions the need for 'deprogramming' a teacher in order to dislocate his or her routines. He also argues the need for the community to recognize that an innovation that requires substantial change of habit is likely to impose on teachers the burden of incompetence while they

---

*Sections of this chapter were given at a conference held at Simon Fraser University in 1980. Bruce Joyce and Ted Aoki (see later) also gave papers. The papers were published in 1984 (see Joyce and Showers, 1984; Aoki, 1984).

experiment with, and learn to feel comfortable with, the new skills. The community must be helped to accept tentativeness and uncertainty during a period of unlearning and new learning. In this way, innovating teachers may sense a context of support, and they may have the nerve to see the innovation through. As Joyce memorably puts it: the community must be understanding of, and tolerant of, the 'socially deviant behaviour' that teachers are likely to exhibit in the early stages of any fairly substantial innovation.

Joyce is here confirming, in vivid fashion, our own experience in the UK of the problems of innovation, but I want to ask . . . Should we not be extending these observations about teachers to pupils? Does not the innovation dislocate the routines of pupils as well as teachers? And is not the dislocation of routine as uneasy an experience for pupils as it is for teachers? And if we need to legitimize teachers' tentativeness and insecurity as new ways of working are introduced in the classroom, should we not also think how to help pupils see that uncertainty and tentativeness may be legitimate – whether it is their own or the teacher's – and that insecurity may be natural to the situation at that point in time?

The thesis that I want to explore is this: that where innovations fail to take root in schools and classrooms, it may be because pupils are guardians of the existing culture, and as such represent a powerful conservative force, and that unless we give attention to the problems that pupils face, we may be overlooking a significant feature of the innovation process. Joyce talks about the community exerting a homeostatic influence on the culture of the school – and he defines the community in terms of parents and administrators. I want to argue that it is the community in the classroom – the pupils – that may be exerting the strongest influence towards stability, and not surprisingly so, if we fail, as we have often done in the past, to involve pupils in understanding the purpose and the process of the change that the teacher or the school is intent on bringing about.

Illustration

Two events lodged in my mind and marked the early stages of my awareness that there was an important issue here. The first event occurred when I visited an open-plan primary school in the UK a few months after it had opened. The pupils had been transferred, with their teachers, from an old Victorian school with dark classrooms and heavy desks and with an atmosphere quite different from the atmosphere of the new school. I talked to the school principal who said that the teachers had adjusted well to the new situation; they had had considerable support in terms of discussions and opportunities to attend courses to prepare them for the transition. But the pupils, it seemed, had had some difficulty: they had started to steal pencils and to hide them away in little squirrel-like caches. The school staff became concerned about this behaviour and met to try to interpret it and plan what to do. Their interpretation was that pupils were missing the sense of possession over space that they had enjoyed in their old school where they worked in their own classrooms and could put their belongings in their own desks. The staff thought that by hiding pencils away in secret places the pupils, who were 6 or 7 years old, would feel that they had a private space in the school which they could think of as their own. The school principal and her staff decided to flood the school with pencils until children felt less under threat by the openness of their environment. I was struck, in this event, by the way in which the problems that the teachers might encounter in this transition had been anticipated, whereas the problems that the pupils might encounter had not.

The next event was a story related to me by a student teacher. It was about her first teaching practice. She was working with a class of 7-year-old pupils in a school that had decided to celebrate the coming of the autumn by holding a harvest festival. The pupils became increasingly excited as they brought in fruit, vegetables, bread and flowers and arranged them in the main hall of the school. Every morning they would ask: 'When will it be harvest festival?' One afternoon, the pupils were taken into the hall where they sat on the floor in rows and listened to the minister who talked to them. The next morning the children continued to ask: 'When will it be harvest festival?' But harvest festival, as the teachers knew, was the occasion of the talk, in the hall, by the minister. The idea in the minds of the teachers, which they had taken for granted, had not been explained to the pupils.

Then there were two experiences of innovation – one mine and the other recorded by Denscombe (1980) – that confirmed my belief in the significance of the issues that lie behind the task of introducing innovation to pupils. I shall recall both experiences in some detail.

Denscombe's study highlights pupils' power to force a compromise on innovation: it is a story of strategy and counter-strategy. Denscombe carried out his observations in a co-educational 14 to 18 community college in which humanities lessons were distinctive for being the fullest expression of the school's policy to move towards a more integrated curriculum and a more integrated social organization. The principle of open teaching, even though it was supported by the rhetoric of school policy, did not affect the high-status subjects in the curriculum where work continued to follow the conventions of closed-classroom teaching and learning. Humanities was 'immediately recognisable as novel and offered a marked contrast with the situation in the vast majority of classrooms'. Pupils' experience of the new style of work was, however, contained, in that in each week pupils spent only 6 out of 33 periods in humanities lessons: 'as a result, the Humanities lessons still constituted something of an abnormal situation'. Denscombe interprets the pupils', and to a lesser extent the teachers', responses in humanities as evidence of an impulse 'to normalise the situation' in terms of experiences elsewhere in the school.

Humanities lessons were held in a hall large enough to hold 60–80 pupils. The resource-based approach supported a fairly high degree of individualized and small group learning. The whole group was only summoned together for lead lessons, which were usually used to introduce a new topic or phase of humanities work. Pupils were, in theory, free to move around the open space, to sit where they wanted, and to discuss their work. The staff saw themselves as catalysts and their attempts to build a collaborative approach were characterized by 'relationships depending on conviviality and friendliness'.

The teachers' way of reducing the dissonance between their practice in humanities and their practice in other lessons was to implement 'a subtle closure on the openness of the work area'. They proceeded to identify themselves closely with a group of pupils and 'consequently re-instituted a significant feature of the closed classroom' (p. 54). A consequence of this move was that pupils were expected to retain membership of a sub-group and sit within it; movement from one group to another, therefore, became conspicuous rather than normal, and could be seen to constitute a threat to the teachers' organizational scheme and to the pattern of social control that it supported.

The re-establishing of some recognizable manifestations of authority and control on the part of the teacher may well have given the lie to the ideal of collaborative relationships that the open teaching approach was designed to develop. It became evident, at least, that pupils were not changing their perceptions of the teaching situation, but were persisting in seeing it as one where they would continue to operate strategies that promoted their own interests at the expense of the teachers' aspirations for them.

The problem, however, was that some of the strategies that were effective in a closed classroom in challenging the teacher's version of order, or in creating some diversion to win a temporary respite from work, were not effective in the open classroom. For example, in the closed classroom, noise, or certain noises, are evidence of the loss of teacher control, and as a classroom strategy, therefore, noise may be consciously generated by pupils 'precisely as a counter to the teacher-invoked pressure to maintain quiet orderliness in the classroom'. However, in humanities, noise was accepted by the teachers as a normal feature of open-plan work. Pupils had, therefore, to develop new strategies, adapted to the characteristics of the open situation. The classroom organization led teachers to move around their 'areas' and spend time talking with individual pupils. The exchanges were friendly but the friendliness itself was not, it seems, without some aspiration towards control, in that it allowed the teacher 'to be privy to the kind of personal information about pupils which they could not glean under less relaxed circumstances' (see also the characteristics of Bernstein's, 1975, 'invisible pedagogies'). Friendliness, therefore, which included 'cultural identification and humour', was an appropriate starting point for counter-strategy. Pupils learned to take advantage of frequent buddy-like chats to redirect or divert the teacher's focus of interest:

Teacher: Robin, you owe me some work. You still haven't handed in the last unit.
Pupil: Well, I had to go out last night . . .
Teacher: That's no excuse . . .
Pupil: No, well . . . it was football . . . City, you know.
Teacher: That's hardly the point . . .
Pupil: Have you seen them recently? They are coming on quite good

now. You know . . . they have got a lot of young lads in the side . . .
good they are.

Teacher: Yes, I hear that the average age of the team is 20 or so.

Pupil: Makes you too old, doesn't it . . .

Teacher: Cheek. I have got a few years left in me yet.

Pupil: Why, where do you play? Must be goal-keeper at your age.

Teacher: Well, actually, if you must know . . .

The pupils had succeeded in protecting themselves from too close a
surveillance!

Another innovative feature of the humanities work was the flexibility of the
course structure – and, again, it became the arena for the development of
counter-strategies by pupils. The course guidelines stated: 'You may inquire
into other aspects of your own or your teacher's choice'. It was therefore
legitimate for pupils to insist that they discuss matters that they found interesting. The 'very interest and relevance of the topics, combined with teacher
tolerance of talk in open classrooms', allowed pupils to spend a lot of time
talking: the loophole was that the boundaries between 'proper work' and
'having a chat' were blurred in a way which pupils were quick to exploit:

Teacher: Jean, Alison, you have been doing a lot of talking. Get on with
some work.

Pupil A: We are talking about the work.

Teacher: I have heard you chatting about clothes . . .

Pupil A: Yes, well that's it, isn't it . . . we are talking about fashions. It is
part of the unit.

Teacher: Still sounds like chat to me. Anyway, how much have you
written? It has got to be written down for the unit . . .

Pupil B: But we have got to discuss things first.

Denscombe concludes that pupils were using the ambiguity of the situation to
avoid work, and that teachers, possibly because they were not monitoring their
new practices, were using familiar control questions to initiate conversation
with the small groups.

Thus, it seems that the potential of humanities as an innovation was not fully
realized. First, teachers made a move that resulted in the fluidity of the large
group being reconstituted as normal classroom groups, not separated by walls
but with what amounted to territorial spaces. Secondly, the collaborative, non-
authoritarian relationships that the humanities teachers were expected to support existed only on the surface of pupil–teacher interaction. The teachers used
the 'new' relationship to find ways of retaining a comfortable feeling of social
control and the pupils reacted by finding out, with an unerring sense of
direction, the weaknesses in the situation and so were able to develop counter-
strategies that gave them opportunities to find levels of work that suited them.
So, while the situation *looked* different, the power relationships and the attitudes that those relationships habitually support remained essentially the same.
The temporarily neutral ground of an innovation had in fact been invaded by

the battle of wits played out in conventional classroom teaching, and there was now little likelihood of the terms of the teaching and learning being renegotiated to bring them more in line with the collaborative ideal of the humanities blueprint. The spirit of innovation was compromise. The question, for me, is this: Would the outcome have been different if the teachers had, together, planned how to introduce and justify the innovation to the pupils and if they had spent more time together clarifying their understanding of the key principles that characterized the innovation?

The last story, which I also want to tell in some detail, relates to a curriculum development project on which I worked as a member of the project's central team. The project was called the Humanities Curriculum Project (HCP, 1971; see Chapter 1). About 4 years after the project was officially over – that is, its period of financial support had ceased and the project was well into its phase of dissemination – Lawrence Stenhouse (the project's director) and I decided that we would like to take a fresh look at the project and we asked the principal of a comprehensive secondary school near the university where we worked whether we could have a group of 14- or 15-year-old pupils for two periods a week for at least two terms. Now, to make sense of this story I have to say something about the project as 'an innovation': it was difficult to understand; it was costly in terms of school resources; it conflicted with the established values of most classrooms. In this project, discussion was the main mode of inquiry and the teacher acted as a neutral chairperson. Discussion was informed and disciplined by evidence; that is, items of material from history, journalism, literature, philosophy, art, photography and statistics might be introduced if they were relevant in order to help the pupils extend the range of their considerations and deepen their understanding of the issue under discussion. The kinds of demands that this curriculum project made on teachers, pupils and schools are summarized below:

New skills for most teachers
1. Discussion rather than instruction.
2. Teacher as neutral chairperson, i.e. not communicating his or her point of view.
3. Teacher talk reduced to about 15 per cent.
4. Teacher handling material from different disciplines.
5. New modes of assessment.

New skills for most pupils
1. Discussion, not argument or debate.
2. Listening to, and talking to, each other, not just to the teacher.
3. Taking initiatives in contributing, not being cued in by teacher.

New content for many classrooms
1. Explorations of controversial social issues, often in sensitive areas (e.g. race relations, poverty, family, relations between the sexes).
2. Evidence reproduced in an original form – no simplification of language.

Organizational demands on schools
1. Small discussion groups, each with a teacher chairperson.
2. Mixed-ability groupings preferred by many schools.
3. Chairs arranged in large circle or rectangle.

The project team put much effort into helping teachers understand the principles of the project through attendance at rigorously planned and intensive residential training courses. Although we were aware that pupils had difficulty in making adjustments to this way of learning, we gave remarkably little attention to the task of helping teachers introduce the innovation to pupils. Our evaluation officer, Barry MacDonald, was aware of the problems, however:

> Teachers do not anticipate the extent to which pupils have developed, in their previous schooling, a trained incapacity for this work, nor the degree to which the pupils have been successfully socialised into a tradition of teacher dominance and custodial attitudes. (MacDonald, 1973, p. 24)

One pupil had commented, memorably:

> All our life, we have been in schools. We've been taught that what the teacher says is right. But when we're in this room doing discussion, it's hard for us to disagree with him after all these years. We sort of come to conform with them.

It was not until I experienced directly, as a teacher in the classroom might experience it, the problem of introducing this innovation to pupils, that I began to appreciate the practical and procedural implications.

Back to my story. Lawrence Stenhouse and I were given a group of twenty 14-year-old pupils for a double period a week – about 70 minutes. The sessions were scheduled on Monday morning immediately before the lunch break. The pupils would normally have been doing English literature. Classes were streamed for some subjects and in the fourth year there were 10 streams. We were given the ninth stream – a mixture of pupils who knew that they were almost bottom but who had not quite given up hope, and pupils who were able but who had in spirit given up school. The teacher who normally taught them was having discipline problems with the group and gladly surrendered them to us. Incidentally, the school had tried the project 6 years earlier but had abandoned it. Project materials were lying dustily in cupboards.

Lawrence and I arrived one Monday morning. A teacher explained to the whole group of pupils that they were to work in smaller groups, one with Mr Stenhouse and one with Miss Rudduck 'from the university'. The group lists were read out. The principle of allocation was not made clear, although we were told later, and the pupils must have known, that all the really unruly pupils were put in Lawrence's group – I had the rest. Our meetings were to be held in the block reserved exclusively for the use of the senior pupils in the school – the 17- and 18-year-olds. Unlike the ordinary classrooms, which had rows of desks, the rooms we were to use were fairly small and had chairs around a central block of tables; the only familiar feature of the new classroom was the blackboard. The pupils we were to work with had so far had no experience in school of working through discussion.

So began our attempt at innovation – under not very auspicious circumstances, but circumstances that many other teachers attempting the innovation would have found themselves facing. We started. Each week I began the session by explaining that I was acting as a chairperson, not a teacher; that discussion was an opportunity to learn from each other and not just from me; that there was evidence which we could use to help the discussion along and give it depth. The group listened, apparently attentively, for this bit was familiar: it was teacher talk. But they didn't ask questions about what I meant nor seemed to relate what I had said to what followed. After a few weeks they had learned to write the title, 'Humanities Curriculum Project', on their folders, and spell it correctly. This again was a familiar achievement.

My acting as a chairperson and sitting at the table alongside the pupils marked a change from the conventional authority-based relationship of teacher and taught. But the pupils had no conception of any alternative convention for they could not realize the form of discussion for a long enough period of time to perceive what the structure of the alternative convention might be. In this limbo world, behaviours that would normally be suppressed, or if expressed would constitute a direct challenge to the authority of the teacher, were given free rein. In adopting the role of the chairperson, I had cut myself off from the usual means of control that the behaviour of the group would certainly have elicited in a normal teaching situation. There was an impulse towards small talk and against this backdrop of perpetual and seemingly mindless motion there stood out a number of attention-seeking incidents that, despite repetition, maintained their appeal. We seemed to have arrived at an impasse in terms of progress with discussion. Maintaining my role was a severe strain. I could understand why teachers might give up. We recorded each discussion on audio-tape and the group was interested in playing back the tape, but only to hear the sound of their own voices or to have a go at being in charge of the technology. There were some achievements in the handling of discussion, but they were not cumulative, and I could not see how to advance the learning in any systematic way. And then came the breakthrough.

One week we invited both our groups down to the university to watch video-tapes of other schools attempting the same style of work. To be honest, I think at the time we had conceived of this as an outing rather than as an opportunity to test an educational hypothesis. It was a relief from the strain of trying to sustain the innovation. The pupils assembled; we gave them coffee and biscuits. The chauvinist impulses that had made it difficult for girls to contribute to the discussion without being ridiculed were now apparent in the social organization of the group. The girls sat at the back, the boys sat near the TV screen and ate the biscuits. The first video-tape we put on was a disaster in that it unwittingly played to these chauvinist tendencies. It was made in an all girls' school. Now, in an all girls' school there is no incentive for girls to display to peers. There they sat on the screen, hair in rather untidy bunches and wearing ordinary pullovers. Our boys had probably never known a situation in class in which there was not an element of sexual awareness: our girls wore black bras under white blouses; their make-up was subtle. The tape represented an unfamiliar and absurd world. We had to take the tape off.

The second video-tape was more productive. Our pupils started to respond, making comments on the size of the group and the seating arrangements – in both cases, similar to the ones we had adopted. They also noted the teacher's generally short and quiet contributions.

The following week, in my group, the climate had changed. Jim was speaking for the group. Jim was the group leader, the guardian of the old regime. I would like to quote a memorable passage from that session. We were discussing an issue within the theme 'relations between the sexes', and considering the circumstance of early marriages and arranged marriages:

> *Jim*: Miss is talking too much and getting interested in the group. As chairman she shouldn't talk, you know, as much, leaving it to the group to argue between themselves. Well, not sort of argue – to talk between themselves and have more discussion between themselves than with the teacher. Because you are, you know, sort of being the chairman and not the teacher.
>
> *Ellen*: Miss, this Indian's mother went back to India and brought back a husband while her daughter was still in the sixth form.
>
> *J.R.*: [An interested response] Really?
>
> *Jim*: There you go again, Miss.
>
> *J.R.*: [Slightly apologetically and rather illogically] I'm trying to ask a question.
>
> *Jim*: Oi, you lot, instead of talking to Miss, talk between us lot. Everything you say, you say to Miss. Why not talk between us lot?

The opinion leader in the group had become the interpreter of the innovation, not the saboteur of the innovation. From that point we made progress, but it was slow for there was no whole-school commitment to the new way of working, and the pupils had no opportunity, therefore, to consolidate the way of working in other lessons.

Reflection

At this point, I should like to review and elaborate on the issues that give meaning to the two accounts. First, there is the acknowledgement that pupils' definitions of school and classroom behaviour can be powerful conservative forces in educational practice. If the norms of classroom behaviour are suddenly changed and a new structure and mode of learning are introduced, then it is not surprising that the pupils might seek to reinstate the familiar, the comfortably predictable, and through the power of pressure lure the teacher back into recognizable routines.

Secondly, we need to think on what basis innovations are introduced to pupils. In Ted Aoki's (1984) words, within the instrumental model of implementation an innovation is likely to be perceived as a new commodity to be dispensed by teachers and consumed by pupils. In such a framework, teachers are likely to construe the introduction of an innovation as the implementation of a set of practices which their authority, or the authority of the school, is sufficient to enforce. Pupils are unlikely to be helped to understand the meaning of the innovation: that is, what the innovation implies for teacher–pupil and pupil–pupil relationships in the classroom; what different behaviours or kinds of achievement will be valued; and the view of knowledge that the innovation endorses. Instead, pupils may have to build up the jigsaw of meaning from the pieces of information that their observation of the teacher's behaviour, over time, will yield – and if pupils do not have the curiosity or patience to puzzle things out, then they may choose instead to resist the innovation and escape from uncertainty by moving back on to the familiar territory of established norms.

An alternative to the imposition of an innovation through the authority of the teacher is to explore the character of the innovation with pupils. What Ted Aoki says fits well: in his practical action model of implementation, he talks about a 'communal venturing forth' to understand the meaning of the new framework in which both teacher and pupils are to work. Indeed, the critical exploration of what meaning is, he says, a precondition of effective acting together.

Thirdly, we have to find a way in which to set up and conduct this critical dialogue. Originally, we had conceptualized the problem in these terms:

> For planned innovation to be successful, the pedagogical model in the minds of the designers of the innovation must become transparently real to the members of the target culture. This is often a staged process. Once the teacher has interpreted the pedagogical model in the minds of the designers of the innovation, the model in the mind of the teacher must become transparently real to the pupils. (Hull and Rudduck, 1981)

Aoki puts it differently: the teacher may invite pupils to enter his or her interpretive framework and sort out the meaning of the innovation in dialogue.

But this is easier said than done. How is it to be achieved? Our experience suggests that explanations of principle are inadequate to convey the meaning of an innovation to pupils if the pupils have no reference points in their past experience that allow them to translate those principles into dynamic behaviours. The pupils whom I had worked with had no shared referent for such abstract terms as 'neutral chairperson', 'discussion', 'pupil initiative', 'reflective inquiry'. They realized these concepts in action almost accidentally, it seemed, from time to time, but they could not sustain the form of learning long enough to analyse it and explore its meaning collaboratively. If an explanation of principles is inadequate, pupils need an illustration of the principles in practice. Hence the shift towards video-tapes of other groups of pupils engaged in work that embodies those principles.

Video-tape, we think, may have two strengths. First, it legitimizes the involvement of pupils and teachers in innovation. They see other groups, in recognizable school settings, behaving in the 'abnormal' way of the innovation. In the often conventional climates of schools, this can be helpful. It is a way of legitimizing what Bruce Joyce (see earlier) called the 'socially deviant behaviour' of an innovation. Secondly, video-tape provides a shared image of the 'strange' behaviour of the innovation that can be analysed by the group, and out of this analysis the group may come to build their own sense of form. What I am trying to say here is that the principles of an innovation are best communicated through a shared experience of the principles in action, and if this cannot be achieved within the group itself, then it may be attempted through a surrogate experience of the principles in action that video-tape can supply.

A broader framework

At this point, I would like to move out from this close-up concern with one small but potentially significant aspect of change in schools and try to fit what I have been talking about into a broader framework.

In this framework, the key concept is culture. Hagerstrand, who has written about the spatial diffusion of innovations from the standpoint of the geographer, defined an innovation as a 'cultural novelty'. This for me was a beguiling definition, but what do we mean by 'culture'? Culture is a social accomplishment; it is learned and shared. Culture is about the capability of the members of a group to act on the basis of a consensus of meanings manifested in linguistic usage and dependent on a deeper consensus of values and understandings (Stenhouse, 1963, p. 122). The power of culture is that it can sustain a complex pattern of norms. We can see that this is so at the level of the classroom from the two anecdotes that I related earlier. Olmsted confirms this is his book, *The Small Group* (1959, p. 84):

> Each group [for instance, a class in a school] has a subculture of its own, a selected and modified version of some parts of the larger culture [for instance, the school] . . . without its own culture no group would be more than a plurality, a congeries of individuals. The common meanings, the definitions of the situation, the norms of belief and behavior — all these go to make up the culture of the group.

This would be true for any other working group. It seems helpful, therefore, to analyse the problems of innovation in terms of cultural change. The task in innovation is to penetrate the existing culture of the group and to create a new culture from within. The main difficulty, as we have seen, is that one cannot establish a temporary cultural vacuum in order to make space for what is new. And, indeed, if one could eliminate the existing culture, there would be no basis for exploring, collaboratively, the meaning of an innovation.

Schwab (in Westbury and Wilkof, 1978, pp. 170–71) captures the essence of the problem:

If the enterprise is to be successful it is the new logic and not some radically mistaken version of it which must be tried. Yet this is the unlikeliest outcome of all. For, if the new logic be described in its own terms, its hearers must struggle hard for understanding by whatever means they have. These means, however, are the old modes of understanding, stemming from the old logic. Inevitably the new will be altered and distorted in this process of communication, converted into some semblance of the old. . . . If the new logic is entirely converted into the terms of the old, a static and unrecognised misunderstanding is likely to result.

Above all, the teacher as the mediator of change must struggle to understand the innovation in its own terms and must struggle to introduce it in its own terms to colleagues and to pupils in the working group. As the partners wrestle with the meaning of the curriculum innovation in their setting, so they build a new classroom culture that reflects new principles of judgement and action. This is dynamic change rather than dynamic conservatism. Schwab describes it in these words, which can apply to a teacher and his or her pupils as well as to a team of teachers working together (in Westbury and Wilkof, 1978, p. 173):

As they [the participants in the innovation] translate their tentative understanding into action, a powerful stimulus to thought and reflection is created. . . . The actions undertaken lead to unexpected consequences, effects on teachers and students, which cry out for explanation. There is reflection on the disparities between ends envisaged and the consequences which actually ensue. . . . The new actions change old habits of thought and observation. . . . Energies are mobilised and new empathies aroused. There then arrives a new and further understanding of the ideas which led to it.

Changing 'old habits of thought and observation' is a crucial stage in the task of introducing innovation.

6 Helping Pupils Manage the Transition to Enquiry-based Learning

'Planned' change, in the days of the curriculum movement, was a phrase that usually signified that the change in question was someone else's idea. Hence the growth of opportunities for teachers to attend in-service courses designed to help them manage the intellectual and practical shifts to new ways of working. In an era of school-based curriculum development, 'planned' change is more likely to mean 'planned by teachers in a particular school'. In either situation, the pupils' right to know what change is about is often neglected.

Given an ideal of curriculum innovation as a collaborative enterprise between teachers and pupils, within what framework might exploration and negotiation of new classroom procedures be initiated? This question (which was posed in Chapter 5) became the starting point for a research project (Hull and Rudduck, 1981) of which one of the constituent studies is reported here: the study of an in-service conference for pupils that was organized to help pupils make an informed transition from instructional teaching to enquiry learning.

An in-service conference for pupils

In our study, we worked with twenty-four 12- to 13-year-old pupils and one teacher from a semi-rural high school. The pupils were a mixed-ability group: 'At the top end are some borderline grammar school pupils, at the other end E.S.N.' Fred, who was head of humanities, planned to introduce a new approach to history with his group of third-year pupils. The approach was to be enquiry-based. He had a clear idea of what he wanted to achieve in the new history course:

> Until now they've been learning history, which is what we call "learning the facts" . . . whereas now I'm really wanting to make them into historians where they start asking questions and start answering their own

questions, and where they come to their own conclusions. . . . I want them to begin to feel that I don't know all the answers. . . . I think they'll also be starting to deal with different materials which they haven't dealt with so far. All the material they've had before has been books, books and me. . . . I also feel that we've got to start teaching them *how* to proceed to answer questions.

To some extent I think the most difficult thing for them to adjust to will be working on their own, not being directed quite so carefully, not so structured. The other thing is, in fact, having to think for themselves. I just don't think they've done this before.

There are very few children who are really able to sit down and conduct an argument – well, not an argument, a dialogue. Maybe this is what happens – it *is* an argument: they take a position [and] they're not prepared to budge from it whatever the logic of the situation. I think often they can't really enter into a dialogue and say: "Yes, that bit of evidence changes my stance." They take their stance and dig their feet in.

Fred also knew what he wanted to achieve through the one-day conference that we were to organize together: its aim was to provide experiences to help pupils change their view of history and history teaching, and make them sensitive to the following issues:

- that teachers and historians disagree about historians' interpretations;
- that written accounts are often confusing, inaccurate and incomplete;
- that we can enter into a dialogue which might or might not establish a common view but which should be based on available evidence.

Our collaboration with Fred was about providing an environment in which this process of change could begin. We planned to start with a one-day conference for the pupils. Fred's comments helped us determine the content and style of the conference, and also gave us some criteria by which to judge its effectiveness.

Preliminary interviews with pupils

I went to the high school to talk to the 24 pupils, who already knew that a new approach to history teaching had been planned and that they were to be following the course with Fred as their teacher. They were interviewed in friendship groups of 2–4 pupils per group, and were released from lessons to take part. The interviews, which lasted between 15 and 20 minutes, were conducted in an empty classroom and were tape-recorded.

The interviews confirmed Fred's claim that the work he planned to introduce was likely to be very different in terms of content and style from what the pupils were used to, not only in history or social studies but in other subjects as well. Asked to say what history was about, pupils tended to offer short, fragmentary responses: 'About the Romans'; 'About the Romans, the Normans and the Anglo-Saxons'; 'Victorian times and Vikings'; 'Things that happened in medieval and Queen Victoria's time'; 'How they built their houses or castles and they had to build them on top of everything else'. Some pupils tried to offer broader conceptualizations: 'Well, it's a while back'; 'History is about things, about how it happened before the last decade, sort of thing, or century'; 'Kings and famous people, things they've done'; 'What was important'. Asked what were the defining qualities of history compared with other subjects, pupils responded in terms of content and method: 'The people that are famous are usually in history – they're always in history – so you know if you get a famous person it must be history'; 'You have to look in books more in history'; 'Teachers talking away and you're not doing anything'. None of the pupils showed any enthusiasm for learning history and the picture that emerged was similar to that reported by the Schools Council (1968).

Pupils' accounts of everyday teaching experiences were fairly consistent across groups. Their capacity to analyse situations outstripped their capacity to articulate what they understood, and many of their responses were simultaneously awkward *and* insightful. Pupils spoke as though they were often becalmed in uncertainty: 'Being left in a classroom for a whole hour and having to write it all up'; 'Writing you don't know how to do'. Pupils for whom 'not knowing' and 'not understanding' are common classroom experiences can be nervous about seeking support from another pupil – 'asking The Brain'. Instead, you sit there 'and try to work it out – yeah, quietly'. Movement to the teacher's desk *is* permissible but 'sometimes you feel you keep botherin' them and they get a bit tired with you'. The hope of the slower pupils, a generous one, and expressed without resentment, was that the teacher 'might try and help the ones what didn't know so much, but get the other ones all right'. In this class, the 'other ones' were in a minority. Another hope was that there might be more time in class to learn things properly: 'You know, instead of just having the top surface and go onto something else, go right into something.' The pupils were not aggressive. They tolerated their classroom work even though some of them could see how it might be improved. The routines, if dreary, were at least predictable, and that meant a certain security.

The one-day conference that we planned took account both of Fred's aspirations for his new course in history and of the pupil's inventory of their present, accepted discontents.

The conference

The conference was held at the university of East Anglia (some 15 miles from the school) in a nineteenth-century barn that had been restored for large occasional events – one-day exhibitions, social evenings, and so on. 'The Barn' is a very large, bare room with a smaller room leading off where food can be stored and crockery washed up. There is a small raised platform in the main hall and doors lead out onto grassy banks that slope down to a river.

Fred had kept the pupils and their parents informed about the purpose of, and arrangements for, the one-day conference. When they arrived in the minibus, the pupils seemed excited but uncertain what 'the university' would be like: 'I thought it would be a sort of classroom'; 'I thought it'd be just a big hall with the teachers up there doing the lecture'. Waiting in the barn were named folders – one for each pupil – containing a copy of the conference programme, a note of the groups they were to work in, some writing paper and a name tag. Six adults were present to work with the pupils: Fred and David from the pupils' school; John, an historian from the local college of education; and Jean, Charlie and Bev from the university. Jean and Charlie were working on the project; Bev had taught history in a local high school and had directed a project in local history. We planned a day of varied activity, with small groups of pupils working first on their own and later with a chairperson, and with plenary sessions to review experience through discussion and through videotape.

Our aspiration was to give the pupils, who were used to instructional teaching, an alternative learning experience. Explanations at the level of principle were unlikely to affect the desired change in learning style – pupils would, we anticipated, have difficulty in translating words into actions. But there were two tasks that we knew were powerful enough to lead pupils into the conventions of enquiry learning. Both tasks had tightly specified ground rules and both were engaging – compulsively so. What they guaranteed was an experience of enquiry learning which, we hoped, the pupils might be able to reflect on and from which they might derive criteria for judging their subsequent performance in history lessons.

The conference consisted of four sessions:

Session 1: Task 1
The day started with a reminder about the purpose of the conference and a briefing for session 1: the seven groups of pupils worked on their own, trying to write some history on the basis of three documents which related to the theft of some hen's eggs in a Suffolk village in 1864. There were sufficient ambiguities across the documents to generate considerable questioning of the status of the evidence. The pupils had about 50 minutes to look at and discuss the documents and then to write their history. It was suggested that each group should appoint one pupil to act as writer.

Session 2: Task 2
The five groups of pupils, each with a chairperson and an assortment of unfamiliar, mainly historical objects, examined the structure of the objects in relation to their possible function, and considered what evidence was available to the group, both in the objects themselves and in pupils' past experience, which might help them to speculate about the period in which an object might have been made, and where and how it might have been used. Finally, each group was to choose one object to talk about to another group and to appoint one pupil to act as spokesperson.

Session 3: Task 1 reviewed
During session 2, the histories written in session 1 were typed out. The pupils
and staff sat in a large circle, each with copies of the histories. A member of each
group was invited to read the group's 'history', and the reading was followed by
questioning and discussion of the group's interpretation of the evidence.

Session 4: Review of the conference
In the final session, the pupils met again in groups, with their chairperson from
session 2, and discussed the conference. The concluding event was the play-
back of parts of the video-tape that had been made during the day as a running
record of the conference. Time was short and the tape was more a way of
rounding-off the day in plenary session rather than an opportunity to analyse
the processes that had been used during the conference sessions.

Evidence of the strength of habit as a brake on change

What did the conference achieve? The transcripts of the groups at work are
evidence of the power of the tasks to provide an experience of enquiry learning
and they are also evidence of the points of tension where the conventions of
the instructional classroom encountered the pull of an alternative set of conventions. The extracts used to illustrate this point are from transcripts of the
session 1 discussions, where the groups were writing their own histories of the
egg-stealing incident. The hope was that the task would encourage pupils to
see that historical sources are often incomplete and confusing, even innaccu-
rate; that writing history is a process that requires interpretation; and that
interpretations can be influenced by personal values and perspectives.

The first extract shows how one group of pupils tried hard to grapple with
the evidence when something puzzled them. The four boys are discussing a
sentence in one of the documents, the account of the egg-stealing incident
from the local newspaper:

> P.: If it lay in the hedge, was it on private property? [Reading] . . . "I
> was watchin' some eggs that lay in the hedge."
> P.: What?
> P.: 'Cause it says . . . look, "Last Wednesday night I was looking at some
> hens' eggs that lay outside Mr Paine's farmyard."
> P.: You see, just *outside*, just *outside* Mr Paine's farmyard. It doesn't say
> just *inside* Mr Paine's farmyard gate. So it might not be on Mr Paine's
> property.
> P.: It's a private roadway.
> P.: That might not have been his private farmyard road . . .
> P.: That means the policeman shouldn't have gone there if it's
> private . . .
> (*Note*: in some recordings we were not able to ascribe names to the
> different speakers.)

But there are also occasions when pupils, having found something in the evidence that they do not understand, accept the first explanation that a member of the group comes up with. Here, another group of boys discuss the same document:

P.: Why should he [i.e. the man accused of stealing the eggs] be going to look after the horses with the eggs in his hand?

P.: Perhaps because . . . I don't know.

P.: He said he wouldn't interfere 'cause he was going after the horses.

P.: With eggs?

P.: Perhaps he was going to have them for his dinner.

A similar rhythm is apparent in the extract from a discussion among three girls:

P.: What's a turnpike?

P.: What's a what?

P.: [Reading] . . . Look: "Near a roadway which runs from a turnpike onto Mr Paine's farm."

P.: Is it a crossroads, or something?

P.: Path?

P.: No. It might be a plant or something.

P.: No, it wouldn't be a plant.

P.: Turnpike? It wouldn't be a river would it?

P.: Yes, a river or something like that.

P.: Yes, a stream.

The last two extracts seem to us to be evidence of a readiness in pupils to seek closure on a problem. This we interpreted as partly due to a habit of mind (pupils are not used to taking responsibility for checking out the logic of their own work) and partly due to a habit of pace (they are used to short periods of time and to finishing the work that has been set). A number of references to time or to completion of the task were made in the different groups. For example:

Sam: What time do we finish?

Dave: A quarter to.

Bob: Do we get marked?

Sam: What's the time now?

Bill: Half past ten.

Sam: Come on, get on with it or we're not going to get done.

Bob: How much more do you think we've got to do?

[A few minutes later]

Bob: When are you going to write it up?

Sam: Right. Shall we write it up now?

Bill: Right. We've got seven minutes to write it up.

These boys had carried over yet another habit from their usual lessons that leads them to 'do' the three documents separately. They do not realize that they should be building their account from the data offered across the three documents; instead, they attempt to summarize each one and therefore miss some of the discrepancies in the data:

> *Dave*: [Looking at another group nearby and whispering] . . . Just imagine how much Alan, Barry, Chris and Rob have done.
> *Bob*: About a line.
> *Sam*: We ain't as thick as them. They've done about as much as us. We can do better . . . [he reads out what he has written] Thomas Edwards was charged with stealing four hen's eggs, the property of Mr J. D. Paine of Risby. Yes . . . [he turns to Bob] Oh, you're doing that one now, are you? . . . [Bob is looking at the newspaper account of the case]
> *Bob*: Yes.
> *Sam*: [To Bob] . . . See. Use your head. Read all of it and get it all done . . . [turning to Dave and Bill] You two should be doing it together 'cause you are looking at the same document.
> [About 15 seconds later]
> *Sam*: Read it. Read it. I'm not doing that document. I'm doing this one.

This impulse towards summary rather than analysis and synthesis leads to an uncritical 'putting it together' exercise at the end of the session. There was some evidence that pupils were prepared to be critical of each other's contributions, but the tone and style of mutual criticism can be difficult to handle without an adult chairperson to set some sort of model. Peer criticism in the small groups tended to show itself as good-humoured ridicule. These boys, you will remember, are summarizing the individual documents:

> *Bob*: [To Sam] Is mine all right? It's crap.
> *Sam*: I don't know, do I? We'll read it in a minute.
> *Bob*: That's a bit crap.
> *Sam*: That don't matter.
> *Bob*: Have a read of it.
> *Sam*: OK . . . [he reads aloud what Bob has written] Last Wednesday night I was watching some hen's eggs which lay . . . [he breaks off] – What do you mean – last Wednesday night? It's only a hundred and eight years ago, you twit.
> *Bob*: I know.
> *Bill*: Last Wednesday night a hundred and eight years ago!
> *Sam*: Hey, you others. Look. He's put last Wednesday night I was watching some eggs. You weren't . . . [laughter] Last Wednesday night. No, don't put that. Put: "A P.C. or something or other put some eggs in the hedge."
> *Dave*: Where does something or other come into it?
> *Bob*: I'll do it again.
> *Sam*: That's all right what you have done, just put . . .
> *Dave*: He's thick.
> *Bob*: Shut yours.

The plenary sharing of the typed and duplicated histories (session 3) provided an opportunity for all pupils to become more analytic of the way evidence might be used. Here, the need to question – indeed the right to question – was communicated and legitimized by the chairperson. It was a memorable, even moving, occasion as pupils, sitting alongside staff in a large circle of chairs, learned to challenge each other's and the staff members' contributions. One girl commented: 'It's silly to go all the way round and never get criticised. You haven't learned anything.'

Overall, this task revealed the children's difficulties in attempting a new way of working and thinking, but the outcomes were also encouraging, showing clearly that pupils, given a carefully planned task, a setting conducive to independent work and a teacher who is sensitive to the principles of enquiry-based work, *can* make progress with a novel form of learning.

The aim of the second task (session 2) was to encourage pupils to explore the interplay of personal experience, knowledge and observation. It was also designed, as with the first task, to help them face uncertainty or inconclusiveness and to accept the notion of 'the best interpretation possible in the light of the evidence available', rather than always to expect the security of known answers. The chairperson's responsibility was to promote collaborative and disciplined questioning of unfamiliar objects and to help pupils reconsider early judgements in the light of later discussion. However, there was considerable variation in the experience of the five groups. Whereas in Task 1 any variation was likely to be due to differences within the pupil groups, here there was an additional variable – the chairperson's interpretation of his or her role.

For example, consider this short extract from one group's work. The group was examining what was in fact an old china inkwell shaped to fit into the hole on the top of a child's school desk. The chairperson is knowledgeable and interested but somewhat dominant and does not use his knowledge to help the group think things out for themselves:

Ch.: Now I won't say a word on this one.

P.: Light bulb . . . [laughter]

P.: What's it got in it?

P.: Is that where the top, where the light comes down from the hole – is it for a light bulb?

Ch.: There's no hole at the bottom is there?

P.: What's in it then?

Ch.: I think it's rubbish. I wouldn't worry about that. It's rather interesting if you can't guess it straight away because I can tell you what that one is – incredibly! Anyone prepared to guess?

P.: Is it easy?

Ch.: Well, when you know, it's quite easy – yes. Perhaps something you don't use so much now. I mustn't give you too many clues . . . [silence] Now, I'll give you one clue. Try to imagine you are in school.

P.: Oh – an ink well.

> *Ch.*: An ink well, it's as simple as that and we're so used to using Biros or things similar. Not so very long ago you were all given pens with nibs and your ink wells were filled and you duly dipped your pen in the ink and you wrote. Now I doubt if they're ever used. There were literally little slits in the top of the desk and your ink well was placed in it and your ink was poured in and off you went. It's an ink well. Well done! We're doing well. That's three we've got isn't it?

Here, the chairperson seems to be encouraging children to guess rather than to pursue their questions through the evidence of the object itself.

Another group was examining a fog horn that had lost its horn. Here, the chairperson was open in relation to knowledge but inclined to control the flow of the enquiry by questions and summaries:

> *Ch.*: Somebody's saying – *you're* saying it's a bellows. *You're* saying it's for the fire. *You're* saying blacksmiths used it. Ian thought it was a bellows as well. Now let's question the evidence we've got. Anything that makes you reconsider that decision? Or anything else you'd need to know about it? Say if it's mucking up your hands because of the dust. OK. Have a look at it, you may be right but we just don't know, you see.
>
> *P.*: . . . comes out at the top.
>
> *Ch.*: The air's coming out at the top?
>
> *P.*: Yes. I've seen one like it before.
>
> *P.*: You'd have to have some sort of . . . [inaudible] . . . pointing it that way.
>
> *P.*: Wouldn't get to the fire though – you'd have to hold it up that way.
>
> *P.*: Upside down?
>
> *P.*: You could use it for blowing smoke up the chimney . . . [laughs].
>
> *P.*: What's this – at this end for?
>
> *P.*: There's a spring for – press it down again.
>
> *P.*: No, that probably pushes.
>
> *P.*: Well, you can, these . . . [touches metal arms] hold it, right? They support it. Well something's got to *give* a little if you press it down. Somethings got to go . . .
>
> *P.*: Probably to fold it up isn't it?
>
> *P.*: You'd have to take all the screws out.
>
> *Ch.*: Let's just summarise a minute. You are saying, Ian, that the spring's there and you've all noticed the spring, but it didn't give much so there's a bit of a problem. And you're suggesting the spring might be there to fold it down but somebody said it's got these stiff arms there, so there's a problem.

This session was due to culminate in an activity that proved particularly difficult for pupils to accomplish. One pupil in each group was asked to present a summary of the group's discussion of one of the objects to another group. Nervousness about a public individual performance clearly deterred pupils from concentrating on the nature of the task:

P.: Well, who's going to do it?

P.: Well, you can remember what people have said and just repeat it to them.

P.: You said you were going to do it.

P.: No, I don't know if I want to do it now.

P.: No, I don't fancy doing it.

The main problem seemed to be the unfamiliarity of offering an account of the group's speculation. The spokesperson's responsibility was to suggest the sequence of his or her group's thinking, including their doubts, the evidence that they considered, the interpretations that they rejected, and the interpretations that seemed acceptable; but, instead, the spokespersons, possibly returning under stress to the security of a more familiar mode of presentation, tended to offer a single conclusion, even where the evidence was too insubstantial to support the conclusion offered or even where the evidence had, in the course of the group's discussion, actually contradicted the conclusion finally offered!

Two months later

So far we have looked at the potential of the conference for providing an experience of a new pedagogy in action. Another area of potential impact was the pupils' perception of history. The pupils were interviewed two months after their day at the university. Meanwhile, they had been doing the 'new' history for two 90-minute sessions a week. It was clear that there had been a shift in perception, but whether this shift was attributable to the conference *and* to the work in history that followed the conference, or mainly to the conference – which was still vividly recalled by the pupils – it was not easy to ascertain. The tasks undertaken in the history lessons, and based on the project *History 13–16*, were certainly not dissimilar to those of the conference sessions in that they included group work based on evidence, discussion, and outings to examine historical monuments.

The post-conference interviews suggested that pupils had developed richer perceptions of history than those they had offered in pre-conference interviews. They had shifted from simple, predictable notions that history is just 'about the past' or 'about Kings and Queens' and 'the Romans' to more subtle conceptualizations: 'Yesterday's History'; 'History is discussing things and discussing people. It's about individual people. How they behave, their personality and everything. What sort of background they come from.'

In the pre-conference interviews, 'historical method' as pupils had experienced it was reading and copying from books, or writing down what the teacher said. That they had shifted their perceptions of the process of historical enquiry was strikingly clear in the post-conference interviews. Now they were using words such as 'investigate', 'understand', 'evidence' and 'proof'. There was a sense of liberation, a readiness to take risks in the classroom and this was clearly a rare experience for these 12 to 13-year-old pupils:

I think you can sort of make your own decision better – it ain't necessary to be right or wrong.

In history it's not a wrong answer sort of thing. Well, there is a correct answer, but you can – teachers haven't got the notes on how it goes so there's not a wrong answer and there's not a right one.

Well, some history doesn't agree. There's not actually an answer.

If I was putting my hand up to say something I wouldn't be worried, something like that.

There were equally committed responses to the idea that history could allow you to 'work things out for yourself':

It's about searching things up for yourself and finding out what *did* happen for yourself, and not through books and that.

You can write down what *you* think.

You're not just doing things out of the book, you're discussing things before you actually write them down, so you understand it.

Pupils' views of group work had also changed since the pre-conference interviews. They were beginning to see that groups weren't just a device for completing a task without making much effort: 'Well, in maths everybody in a group copies, like. They may not understand it. You know, people who don't understand it, copy.' Now they saw collaboration within the group as a means of advancing their learning: 'Over one point three people say something and you have to listen to other people's – you have to listen to what three people thought.' The strategy that the groups were using was one they had experienced in the first session of the conference and it had involved them in the allocation of tasks within the small working groups:

I put it together and he copies it down. That's how we done it at the university.

I usually do the roughing out thing. They choose their parts. Then we have discussion.

Sue reads it out. Linda writes it up. Me and Sharon puzzle it out.

Roles are allocated on the basis of crude estimates – firmly fixed in the peer-group subculture – of 'brains', and competence in reading or writing.

Unfortunately, the simultaneous demands of research in other field settings prevented us from supplementing the interviews with observations of classroom practice.

Reflections on the conference

A major shortcoming of our study was its failure to support the teacher and pupils in maximizing the achievement of the conference by bringing what the pupils had learned enactively under symbolic control. No-one – neither research workers nor teacher – helped the pupils to translate what they had experienced at the conference into an articulate awareness of the principles of the new pedagogy. The conference programme had included opportunities for pupils to review their work, but these proved, in practice, to be an extension of the pupils' enactive encounter with the new pedagogy rather than occasions for criticial reflection.

Back at school, Fred reported regression over time rather than progress. The technique he used to sustain the impact of the conference was re-enforcement of the learning style through involving pupils in tasks similar to those worked through at the conference. However, pupils tended to compare the back-at-school tasks unfavourably with the conference tasks: the conference tasks were highly satisfying in themselves and took a greater lustre from the excitement of the day's outing; they had intensity of focus and were designed as self-contained, single-session activities, whereas the classroom tasks, which tended to span several lessons, lost impact, and the pupils, failing to see the logic of the task, showed a slackening of commitment. For example, asked what they had been doing in history since the conference, pupils offered the following rather vague response: 'This man who got killed and – Richard. Was it the first or second?'; 'Maps, and about blokes that have died and that sort of thing.' In comparison, the task that involved them in writing their own histories of Thomas Edwards and the hens' eggs remained vivid and coherent in their minds.

It was almost inevitable that in the familiar setting of the classroom, and within the framework of conventional timetabling, the impetus generated by the conference would to some extent fall away. Moreover, a teacher working alone, however well intentioned, will have difficulty in sustaining a new teaching style unless criteria are being pressed by colleagues or by pupils. The pupils noticed – but did not discuss with their teacher – occasional shortcomings in the new teaching style: 'When we first started we didn't do any writing – no writing at all. He just talked to us'. The pupils were not able to go further. What *they* lacked was a shared language for talking about the new pedagogy, the reflexive language of critique that seems to come from the analysis of oneself and one's peers at work. Had we helped the teacher to use the video-tapes of the conference discussions as a basis for analysing the characteristics of the new learning and to derive from them a set of criteria that would have served the development of the pupils' subsequent performance as enquirer-historians, the achievement of the conference might have been more firmly sustained. Alternatively, we might have offered to video-tape the pupils at work during the history lessons that immediately followed the conference, so that they could compare the experiences of the conference with the post-conference activities. In this way, they might have established a set of criteria to guide the continuing improvement of their performance in enquiry-based learning. And from such a process there might have emerged the readiness, and the words, to talk publicly about learning.

We concluded that the possibilities and problems of in-service conferences for pupils are similar to those organized for their teachers (see Rudduck, 1981). However successful a conference may be in generating enthusiasm for an innovation, in deepening understanding of what it entails, and in developing appropriate skills, the problem remains of sustaining the impetus generated in one setting in the setting to which the participants return – which may be very different in character and climate. Teachers who attend curriculum conferences that are held away from school come back to a working context mapped by powerful conventions, some – or many – of which may be at odds with the principles of the innovation. The problem is, therefore, to harness the potential of the conference in the everyday professional worlds of the people who attend. The conference is like a cultural island; it is often far removed, geographically and stylistically, from the mainland habitats of the conference members, and thought has to be given to the ways in which the experience of the cultural island of the conference can feed the activity of the mainland habitat, the classroom.

The great strength of the off-site conference, however, is that the excitement that it generates can facilitate and legitimize a radically new practice. In a sense, it performs the same function as a ceremony or *rite de passage* – liberating the participants from the constraints of their familiar past. All but two of the adults-in-charge at our conference could claim innocence both of the culture of the classroom as the pupils knew it and of the classroom biographies of individual pupils: the effect was to free the pupils from their established roles and styles and enable them to explore alternatives. As the conference was so short, however, the potential for change was not carried through, and we can see where habit persists and where it gives way to the demands of new pedagogy.

7 The Right to Question and the Right to Understand the Structures of Learning*

One of the teachers with whom I worked, Maggie Gracie, was known to her pupils as 'the hypothesis teacher'. This was a tribute to her capacity to stimulate hypothetical thinking within the social studies curriculum, Man: A Course of Study (MACOS), which, under the inspiration of Jerome Bruner, reached after a framework to support children in inquiring into the nature of humanness. The label was said to have originated at a parent–teacher meeting when a parent asked to meet the teacher who was in charge of the new subject, 'hypothesis'. The event, now apocryphal, was a result of the way Maggie interpreted, in the reality of her classroom, the rhetoric of the teacher's responsibility, in MACOS, to 'legitimize the search'.

One of the strengths of MACOS materials is that they do not talk down to pupils: pupils are helped to work, from the beginning of the course, within the deep structure of the subject, finding their way with the assistance of a conceptual framework that anthropologists might use to organize and make sense of their experience in the field. Some teachers consider the language of MACOS too difficult for 10-year-olds, but their inability to cope should not be assumed; it is something that has to be tested in practice. And, after all, the vocabulary of MACOS is no more daunting than, say, the vocabulary of the motor car, which many younger children become fluent in outside of school when their curiosity feeds their need to name things and to communicate. Maggie went beyond the invitation to pupils to share the vocabulary of the anthropologist and confronted children with the vocabulary of research and inquiry itself: curiosities found expression in questions, questions took on the action commitment of hypotheses. Individual children would be encouraged to generate and pursue their own hypotheses, however idiosyncratic, for Maggie protected personal meanings, accepting the mystery of a young mind that asked 'Is grass stronger than man?' Questions and hypotheses might also spring out of a curiosity that was nurtured by the exchanges of a working group of children.

*The original chapter was written as a tribute to Maggie Gracie after her early death in 1982.

What mattered was that the children, as individuals or as a group, felt that they owned their hypotheses, could talk about them with some understanding of what the term stood for, and were prepared to be speculative.

Over time, the story of Maggie and the parent–teacher meeting was polished and shaped until what it signified was so familiar to those of us on the MACOS circuit that we only needed to say to each other 'the hypothesis teacher' to remind ourselves of the need to take seriously the intellectual rights of children. The greatest compromise we can allow ourselves to make, if ideas are difficult, is what Bruner calls 'a courteous translation', but sometimes children can manage without even this prop: our aspiration must always be 'to probe by experiment how far ordinary pupils can in fact be taken' (Schools Council, 1965, para. 61).

Many people shared Maggie's concern that in teaching we should respect the individuality of a child's experience and spirit of enquiry, and that we should also struggle to communicate with children about the school's or the teacher's plans so that they can understand what they are doing and why they are doing it. It is the second of these two aspirations that I want to discuss here, drawing on work that local teachers have carried out and that reflects the values that guided Maggie's work in the classrooms of the schools she taught in.

Two examples

In MACOS, the teacher aspires to be a 'model of a learner' and this is difficult enough, but there are other modellings that are important and that have received less attention:

> . . . it appears that children know relatively little about how a teacher thinks about the classroom; that is, what the teacher takes into account, the alternatives the teacher thinks about, the things that puzzle the teacher about children and about learning, what the teacher does when unsure of what should be done, how the teacher feels when he or she does something wrong. There is quite a bit that goes on in a teacher's head that is never made public to children . . . there is a good deal of anecdotal evidence [that] strongly indicates that the more a teacher can make his or her own thinking public and subject for discussion – in the same way we expect of children – the more interesting and stimulating the classroom becomes for students. (Sarason, 1982, p. 225)

I am interested in the ways in which the thinking of a teacher, of a team of teachers, or of a school staff can be made accessible to pupils, both in the ordinary routines of a timetabled term and at times of planned change when routine gives way to novelty.

The right to understand the syllabus

Sarason (1982, pp. 27, 96–7) points to the way in which taken-for-granted 'regularities' in the structure of schooling prevent us from questioning their logic. One example (not discussed by Sarason) is the timetable. A timetable is a synopsis of an exercise in curriculum planning that offers practical information to pupils – what a pupil will receive, where, when, in whose company and for how long. A timetable does not disclose the intellectual logic (or the practical compromises) that influenced its structuring, nor does it communicate the purposes of the courses of study that the pupil is detailed to follow. Pupils accept the timetable as it is given: that is all you know in the classroom and all you need to know.

Peter was a geography teacher in a secondary school. Being part of a research group of local teachers enabled him to distance himself from the routines of schooling and thereby to perceive some of them as problematic. He became interested in the relationship between the timetable, which is what the pupil is given to work to, and the syllabus, which is what the individual subject teacher works from. The teacher, of course, knows what lies ahead, but for the pupils the syllabus unfolds lesson by lesson (in the same way that the year unfolds when you tear a page, day by day, from a block calendar). As a result, what gives point to lessons is less a shared understanding of the course of study as a whole than an awareness of the timing of particular events, like tests and examinations. Peter wanted to try sharing his understanding of a term's work, as represented by the syllabus, with his pupils. Interestingly, the majority rejected his attempt. (Peter's work, which was documented by Charles Hull, is described more fully in Hull *et al.*, 1985.)

What he did was to produce a mini-syllabus of one term's work, which he duplicated and gave to every child in the class. He commented:

> I introduced this document to the group and told them that there were two reasons for preparing the mini-syllabus for them: first to give them an opportunity to prepare work for lessons in advance, to do any background reading they wanted . . . second, so that they would have an idea of the direction in which the day to day work was leading them. I emphasised that the mini-syllabus was designed to enable them to improve their general knowledge of the subject and to understand the rationale of their course of study.

The pupils' responses revealed the extent to which they had been socialized into a view of teaching and learning that did not include the idea of pupils having a right to be informed about the curriculum plan that they were following.

At first – and understandably – there was some resistance to the move, for some pupils saw it as a means of getting them to do extra work. Others were suspicious of the format of the syllabus because they had never seen anything like it before. A few members of the group used it and brought their own evidence into lessons. After 4 weeks, Peter discussed the syllabus with the pupils. A majority had already lost their copy. Several of those who had lost it or who admitted that they had it but never looked at it said, as though in justification, that they did not have anything like it in other subjects. Only three pupils said that they liked having the syllabus because they liked knowing what they would be doing later in the term. Peter commented:

> I became aware of the extent of their conservatism – and their resistance to the novel. This went beyond what I would have expected given that the novelty consisted only of a syllabus. . . . I concluded that by the second year of secondary education pupils value the comfort of familiar techniques and responsibilities . . . expectations are firmly set.

These expectations do not seem to include a pupil's right to know why a course of study is sequenced as it is and what it is leading to.

Peter's attempt to make available to pupils something that is customarily regarded as 'teacher knowledge' was unsuccessful, but the reasons why it was unsuccessful merely serve to underline the importance of the attempt.

The right to understand what assessment is about

The task of a subject teacher, one might reasonably claim, is to help pupils understand and operate the criteria by which work of quality is judged within a discipline or field: for instance, the criteria by which an artist might judge a portrait miniature, an athlete might judge an attempt at a high jump, or the criteria that would guide an historian in selecting and criticizing evidence in relation to an issue. Children's interpretations of such criteria are usually implicit in their work products (essays, paintings, etc.) or in their performances (in games, music, drama, etc.). I shall concentrate here on work products rather than on performances.

The working group of pupils and teacher may spend time explicitly discussing criteria, but pressure to cover the syllabus often prevents this kind of exploration, and pressure from relentless rounds of evening marking makes it difficult for the teacher to offer an extended commentary on individual work products which would enable a pupil both to see where his or her work falls short of the criteria the teacher is using and to find out to what extent his or her understanding of the criteria matches what is in the teacher's mind. Instead, the teacher is often obliged to return sets of pupils' work with technical errors pointed out or corrected and with a final overall judgement expressed as a numerical mark (6/10), grade (C+) and/or a short statement ('Quite good: your work is improving'). The criteria that inform the teacher's overall judgement of a piece of submitted work are not usually made explicit to the pupil except in relation to standards of technical competence – punctuation, spelling, etc.; response to the quality or logic of the pupil's thinking are less easy to communicate and tend therefore to remain implicit.[1]

Several questions follow:

- In what ways can criteria for judging the quality of work be effectively communicated to pupils? (I am ignoring, here, the issue of criteria being negotiated within the working group.)

- In what ways can pupils be helped to deepen their understanding of the criteria?
- In what ways can pupils be helped to critique their own and each other's work in the light of a shared understanding of appropriate criteria?
- In what ways can the teacher monitor the mutuality of understanding of the process of assessment within a working group?

Ian, an art teacher, was curious about these issues and when he joined the staff of a middle school he decided to try out an idea for opening up the assessment process to pupils. During the course of the school year, each class had one term of art, one term of woodwork or metalwork, and one term of food and fabric study. In order to sustain his experiment with assessment, Ian had to seek the support of colleagues responsible for the other subjects. While they agreed to operate his scheme, his colleagues were either not wholly committed to the challenge of changing their marking habits, or they did not fully appreciate the principles that lay behind Ian's approach. Ian himself had difficulty in finding the time to sustain the support for colleagues that the approach required. The idea, however, has great potential. It centred on the provision of 'record books'. Each pupil, in each year of the school, had a notebook that was to be ruled into columns. When a piece of work was started, the date and title, or task, were entered in one column (the finishing date was also entered); in another column, the pupils were asked to offer a critique of the finished work and propose the grade they thought their work merited. On the facing page, the teacher offered his or her critique of the finished work and gave a grade. Where there was divergence between the pupil's and the teacher's analytic commentary and grade, then the teacher had to find time to have a conversation with the pupil about the work and the ways in which it might be looked at and judged.

There are several likely benefits of such an approach: first, an opportunity is provided for pupils to get inside the assessment process and learn how to take responsibility for monitoring the standard of their own work; secondly, an opportunity is provided for pupils to build a language of critique that would enable them to discuss their work 'professionally'; thirdly, an opportunity is provided to see that a grade is a summary of the teacher's perception of the relationship of a particular piece of work to a set of public criteria; and, fourthly, an opportunity is provided for pupils to see how their work develops over time. I looked at a selection of record books of first- and third-year pupils during the second term of the scheme's introduction and was able to see evidence of the scheme's potential. I reflected on how, normally, the strength of the conventions of marking prevents the process of assessment from being a proper support for learning.

The first thing I noted was that under the influence of the comments provided by the art teacher, the pupils were learning to move from descriptive accounts of their work towards critical responses to their work. First-year pupils (9-year-olds) tended at first to offer explanations of content or method rather than analyses. Here are two fairly typical early entries (spelling errors have been corrected):

In my picture I had a frog and pond weed. The pond weed was made of green tissue paper and the frog was made of a dark green plastic bag. I used glue. I cut the frog and the pond weed.

In my picture I used paints and sometimes I mixed colours. The thing that happened to me was that I was just getting into bed when I saw spots on my legs. I asked my mum what they were and she said they were chickenpox. The next morning I had even more spots. The picture I drew and painted had a green and blue bed and a window and blue curtains. I had in my picture a dressing table which was brown.

The problem for third-year students was different. They had already been firmly socialized into thinking that an appropriate comment for them to make on their work was the kind of comment – a global judgement – that teachers generally make:

Quite good but it could have been better.
I enjoyed painting very much but I think I could have done better.
A good topic to do but mine was a bit messy. It could have been better, but I enjoyed painting it.
It was quite good.
It was a good effort and showed how difficult it was.

What Ian had to provide for both the first- and third-year pupils was a model commentary that would help them to think why and in what respects a piece of work was 'good' and in what respects it disappointed them. There was evidence in the record books that pupils were fairly quick to imitate the model provided by their teacher and that a new style of response could quickly become legitimate. Here are two comments that seemed to be transitional:

Quite good because I had used different methods of painting and it looked attractive. (First-year pupil)

My picture is about when I was a World War I German fighter and got shot down on an island where dinosaurs live. The brown doesn't show up much with the red but you can see what it is. The paints have gone runny and have gone where I didn't want them to go. I enjoyed doing this picture very much. I think that I cannot do any better than that picture which I have just done. (Third-year pupil)

However, if pupils are to feel at ease with the new style, and to develop their capacity to write articulately about their work, then the modelling needs to be sustained. This proved difficult. Even Ian, under the pressure of time, sometimes reverted to short and rather conventional written comments and one of his colleagues wrote comments that were consistently conventional, thus recalling past practice. It was noticeable, again, that even pupils who had started to offer more analytic comments to Ian quickly reverted, in term 2, to the familiar style of commentary under the influence of the second teacher's mode of response:

Fairly well executed. A good effort. B− (Teacher)
Could of been better painted. B+ (Third-year pupil)
Quite well completed. B (Teacher)
It was quite good. (No grade given) (Third-year pupil)

There were, in addition, some intrinsic drawbacks to the scheme but none so serious as to negate its clear potential. For example, one pupil used the space for commentary to give himself the kind of glowing praise that he apparently never received from a teacher. He wrote, on an early piece of work, the following eulogy: 'It was a fantastic dream and it was magnificently painted and crayoned and charcoaled and coloured.' Another problem was thown up by pupils who had difficulty in expressing responses in writing that Ian could comprehend. Here is an example:

I was on a ship and the ship was hub in for a big les. I jp lfr bod into the sea and i swam to a wod. I employeb it beure much bot I fot I caud bow it butt.

Our interpretation: I was on a ship and the ship was heading for . . . I jumped overboard into the sea and I swam to a wood. I enjoyed it very much (i.e. painting the picture) but I thought I could do it better.

This pupil, who also had difficulty in reading the teacher's commentary, needed the support of assessment offered and explored in conversation.

Where an innovation is no more than an island in a sea of deeply founded convention, then its chance of establishing itself is fragile. However, the attempt to find a practice that supports the student's right to understand, and learn from, the process of assessment was laudable. Survival, here, depended on Ian's stamina keeping faith with the principles that he was trying to operate, and his capacity to help his colleagues understand those principles and be prepared to test them experimentally.

Ian and Peter, in their own corners of the field and in their own ways, were engaged in the same battle as Maggie: a battle for the intellectual rights of children. Neither was interested, at that time, in anything as controversial as negotiating the content of the curriculum with their pupils. Peter wanted, simply, to ensure that his pupils had some idea of what the term's work in his subject looked like so that they could see individual lessons as part of a coherent whole and could prepare themselves more effectively. He was disturbed by their ready acceptance of the school's policy of disclosing very little of the logic and direction of its curriculum plans to the people − the pupils − who were most affected by them. Ian, for his part, was struck by pupils' equally ready acceptance of the one-sidedness of conventional marking procedures and by the practice they tend to induce in pupils of responding to the grade itself rather than to the complex judgement it represents so that they can confidently take responsibility for the improvement of their own work.

Given the traditions of our education system it is not easy to help young people gain power through understanding. It is important, therefore, that we express our commitment in whatever way we can given the particularities of the context in which we are working. That means recognizing and seizing 'the positive moment that exists amid the cracks and disjunctions created by oppositional forces that are only partially realised in the schools' (Giroux, 1981, p. 31). That, as I interpret their work, is what Maggie, Peter and Ian were all trying to do.

Note

1. This chapter was written before Records of Achievement were introduced which do provide opportunities for dialogue about work.

PART 4

Teacher Involvement and Understanding

Introduction

In a keynote address delivered at the American Educational Research Association Conference in San Francisco in 1989, John Goodlad said that the important concerns of educational research are, first, to understand schools and, secondly, to change them. You cannot do much of the second without the first, he wisely added. Teachers are obviously well positioned to understand schools, but by virtue of the pressures bearing on the school as a workplace, their understanding tends often to be partial rather than comprehensive and opportunistic rather than systematically developed.

No single curriculum development project can be relied on to effect major changes within a single school in the overall social relationships of teaching and learning and to establish and reinforce 'alternative habits of thought and disposition'[1]. In order to counter the weight of convention and expectation, teachers will need, both individually and communally:

1. To try to understand the foundation of their own educational values.
2. To understand, in relation to these values, what change means for them and to be clear what the basis of their individual commitment is.
3. To be prepared to tackle issues of value collaboratively, for unless there is exploration of values and purposes in working groups, coherent whole-school change is unlikely to be achieved.

Chapter 8 looks at the way that individual teachers might use biographical reflection to help them bring back into focus their aspirations for the young people they teach − a process of reaffirmation or even discovery that enables teachers to feel that they are in a position to act on a situation rather than merely to react to it. Chapter 9 asserts the importance of teachers using research as a way of structuring their attempts to 'see' what is happening in their classrooms and in their schools: research has the advantage of providing a set of unfamiliar perspectives that enable the teacher to try to look at the familiar with the eyes of the stranger. Chapter 10 recognizes the power of routine to shape perception and practice and offers the idea of a sympathetic outsider to act as the alter-ego researcher whose task it is to work on the teacher's agenda of concerns and use focused dialogue as a means of extending understanding of classroom events and interactions. Chapter 10 also underlines the importance of working with student teachers to establish the habit of using enquiry and dialogue to keep understanding alive.

Finally, Chapter 11 outlines the story of one school district's attempts to move its schools towards radical curriculum reform. If teachers are to lead change rather than be led by it, it is important that they can commit themselves to the meaning that a particular innovation has for them and for their school. But it is also important that they are sensitive to the complexities of the process of change and in particular the ways in which institutional power structures and individual human anxieties make whole-school transformation difficult to accomplish.

Note

1. The phrase 'alternative habits of thought and disposition', which appears in the title and text of Chapter 12, is from Giroux.

8 Ownership as the Basis of Individual Commitment to Change

> We deal with people's lives – not only the lives of young people but of teachers. . . . We deliberately try to change them and seldom exactly as they would change themselves. We interfere with their lives convinced we are helping them to something better. (Stake, 1987, p. 56)

The potential for professional development can be at its most powerful in a context of change, particularly when teachers understand and are committed to the values that give meaning to the change. But in order to commit themselves to a particular programme of change, teachers may need to reflect, perhaps in a quasi-autobiographical way, on their own past experiences of schooling and higher education, and on their experiences of teaching. By doing so, they may be able to reaffirm or restate the principles that guide their practice, and see what it is they wish to change and why. Teachers who can claim to 'own the problem of change' are those who recognize a potentially creative dissonance that they are prepared to confront and deal with.

The malaise of professionals is, as Schon (1983) says, that they are vulnerable to the dulling effects of routinization. Bruner (1986, p. 22) talks about the need to make the familiar strange 'so as to overcome automatic reading':

> . . . the nervous system stores models of the world that, so to speak, spin a little faster than the world goes. If what impinges on us conforms to expectancy, to the predicted state of the model, we may let our attention flag a little, look elsewhere, even go to sleep. (ibid., p. 46)

Consequently, it is difficult, as Garver (1984) points out, to sustain 'the art of problemation': blind habit, he continues, is a strategy for avoiding deliberation, 'for living in a practical world without in fact acting practically upon it'. Practitioners can easily lose their sense of vision or their capacity for constructive discontent. An important dimension of professionalism is the desire to go on extending one's knowledge and refining one's skills. Both vision and discontent can provide the stimulus. Teachers who are in search of excellence (to borrow a phrase) are likely to be those who are committed to deepening their own professional understanding while pursuing a clear set of educational values.

The situation in the late 1980s was made more complex because we were dealing not just with the normal occupational hazard of routinization, but also with the problem of a widespread and profound sense of disorientation and deprofessionalization among teachers. Preliminary discussions of the findings of an ESRC Teacher Education Project (Poppleton, 1988a, b) suggest that there is a disturbingly high level of dissatisfaction among teachers who have 13 or more years of service. The survey data are confirmed by data from individual and group interviews. There is a strong sense of teachers being pinned against the wall by accusations that education has betrayed the nation, and of being exhausted by the demands of multiple initiatives whose coherence and whose relationship to their own values they haven't the time, and sometimes the energy, to work out. They speak of themselves as a core of veterans who are being used as work horses, set to plough the public allotment of the curriculum rather than expertly to cultivate its secret gardens. The pressures could result in what Poppleton has called 'a militant conservatism', characterized by perspectives that are both anti-bureaucracy *and* anti-innovation. The situation is, ironically, much as Scheffler (1968) described it in the era of teacher-proof curricula: teachers are in danger of assuming the role of 'minor technicians within an industrial process' where the 'overall goals . . . [are] set in advance in terms of national needs' (pp. 5–6, quoted in Smyth, 1987b, p. 3).

Change and the individual practitioner

Real curriculum development (that is, in the present climate, development that allows itself to engage with the fundamental values of equality of opportunity and independence of thought) will not be achieved by teachers who feel so used and acted upon. They have got to feel some control over the situation and, in order to feel a sense of control, they have to recognize what it is in schools, classrooms and in themselves that they want to change. They have to understand, at the level of principle, what they are trying to achieve, why they are trying to achieve it, and how any new possibilities might match the logic of their analysis of the need for change. It is not easy, however, to help teachers to arrive at such complex understandings. First, the teaching profession does not often allow time for, and its culture does not normally support, either communal reflection on practice or discussion of basic philosophies. As Nias (1984, p. 14) reminds us: 'Many of the profession seem to receive little significant assistance in the working out of their own professional values.' Moreover, it is difficult to get an analytic grip on a situation that we have been so effortlessly socialized into. Indeed, as Grumet (1981) says, we are not only part of it, but we are also responsible for it through our constant reconstruction of it:

It is we who have raised our hands before speaking, who have learned to hear only one voice at a time and to look past the backs of the heads of our peers to the eyes of the adults in authority. It is we who have learned to offer answers rather than questions, not to make people feel uncomfortable, to tailor enquiry to bells and buzzers. (Grumet, 1981, p. 122)

If we accept that practitioners' own sense of self is deeply embedded in their teaching, it should not surprise us that they find real change difficult to contemplate and accomplish. They are more likely to seek to extricate themselves from the complex webs of habit if they are powerfully motivated by an awareness that the values they hold dear are not being respected and if, as Sarason (1982, p. 30, quoted in Fullan, 1982, p. 18) says, they are 'hurting' because of the existing curriculum or because of pupils' response to it. Without the sense of 'hurting' as a stimulus to changing the situation, individuals may feel that they are too implicated in past perspectives and present practices to move.

Dealing with the individual's reaction to the possibility of change is not something that has attracted much attention in the literature on educational innovation. We have to go outside education to find any sustained exploration of what change means for individuals: to Marris (1975), for instance, who describes the sense of loss in change as an experience akin to bereavement. Bereavement removes part of the substance and structure of one's familiar and reassuring personal world:

Occupational identity represents the accumulated wisdom of how to handle the job derived from their own experience and the experience of all who have had the job before or share it with them. Change threatens to invalidate this experience, robbing them of the skills they have learned and confusing their purposes, upsetting the subtle rationalisations and compensations by which they reconciled the different aspects of the situation. (Marris, 1975, p. 16)

In order to cope with the disorientations and upheavals that threaten professional status and confidence, individuals need to feel that change is not something that happens to them, and which they cannot control, like bereavement, but instead something which they are in principle seeking and welcoming. Fullan (1982, pp. 28–33) points out that in the initial stages of imposed innovations, teachers are often as much concerned with how the change will affect them personally as about its educational justifications. On reflection, although this preoccupation might seem irritating to those bent on speeding the process of change, the teachers' reactions are understandable. They may not have been helped to prepare themselves for change and to work out in what ways they are, or are not, receptive to it and what it might offer them or their pupils.

I would want to argue that most teachers, given the opportunity to reflect on their experience, would find some 'hurt' that routine or overload leads them to endure rather than to examine. Consciousness of the hurt is most likely to recur as teachers refocus their professional values and goals, admit their political consciousness, and recognize any disturbing gaps between aspiration and present experience. The hurt may be expressed in simple but none the less forceful terms.

Take for example three teachers, Richard, Vic and Ross, who recently joined a university-based development project that was focusing on new teaching and learning strategies in science in the secondary curriculum. Each one opted to join the team because he had, as it turned out, already experienced the 'hurting', although none had, until interviewed, fully articulated and understood the basis of that hurt. All three were from comprehensive schools. One said that his science teaching was reaching only a few pupils and that most of those were very able and going on to higher education. He thought that science was elitist and serving the needs of only a minority of those in secondary schools. For most it wasn't anything that would stay with them and serve them in their later lives. He said that he tried to be the best showman in the world, 'would sweat blood' to entertain them and involve them, but that when he assessed the pupils' understanding it was often poor. Another teacher said that he was becoming increasingly frustrated because some children were not responding to his approach: it was either going over their heads or they were just not switching on in his lessons. Things that had once been successful were not so any longer. He felt that 'something was adrift' in his science teaching. The third said that he was burning up so much energy but seeing so little satisfaction in the children. He wanted them to get involved in science in ways that would not destroy their autonomy and their capacity to develop independence of thought. He wanted them to see the consequences of science for themselves and for society. He wanted pupils to see that there is controversy at the heart of science and that science is not always a subject that is 'right' and that is 'objective'.

If we are interested in substantial curriculum change, we may need to find structures and resources to help teachers to re-examine their purposes, as these teachers did (see Appendix to this chapter), slough off the skin of socialization, and feel more in control of their own professional purposes and direction. Some sense of ownership of the agenda for action is a good basis for professional development and professional learning. Toogood (1989, p. 98) has argued, bluntly, 'Education, I propose, is about self-determination', and Smyth (1987b, pp. 28–9) has suggested that one's career can be seen as part of 'an open-ended search for identity'. As such it can be useful to sort out not only one's values, beliefs, motives, but also to give more attention to the analysis of the experiences of the classroom: 'new perceptions' may lead to 'altered conceptions and reconstruals' of aspects of the art of teaching. They conclude that reflection on one's everyday professional world 'seems an important entry to a deeper understanding of educational innovation and change'. Through such reflection and revaluation the teacher may gain a clearer sense of the way in which the past shapes and informs possibilities for action in the present (Strauss, 1977, p. 104).

The contribution of the biographical approach

The interviews that I conducted with the teachers who joined our science project were not sufficiently penetrating and prolonged to constitute a good example of 'the biographical method' (see Woods, 1985), but they did, I think, help each teacher to organize his own thoughts and feel in command of the problem of change and, later, to be committed to exploring the particular strategy for change that emerged from the project team's discussions. The interviews provided an opportunity for what Apple (1975, p. 127, quoted in Smyth, 1987b, p. 20) describes as 'a serious in-depth search' for alternatives to what is seen with 'the almost unconscious lenses we [normally] employ'. The interviews were a way of both legitimizing the teachers' search and of marking their progress in the enquiry. Thirty years ago, Polanyi (1958, p. 143) wrote:

> Having made a discovery I shall never see the world again as before. My eyes have become different; I have made myself into a person seeing and thinking differently.

This feeling was echoed by one of the teachers who said this just before the end of his period of secondment to the project:

> I feel that having had time to talk and stand back, I now see the important things that are going on in school more clearly than I did when I was right in the thick of it. I think these are lasting perceptions. They are not going to disappear.

Such claims are important, although they may not go quite as far as Lawn (1989, p. 157) suggested:

> A teacher's personal history [can be] compared with another's to develop a critique of institutional constraints and the possibilities of change. This form of schoolwork research is . . . practical, change-based, supportive and reflective. It builds from life history to institutional structures. It aims to emancipate from isolation and from institution.

In this project, we used the biographical framework as a way of helping other teachers to identify with the teachers who undertook the preliminary experimental work – not as a way of leading other teachers to the same outcomes but as a way of encouraging them to ask the questions that these teachers asked about their own past and present teaching and values. Our theory of change suggests that teachers might often be encouraged to analyse their own need for change if they can be in touch – even through print – with teachers who have gone through the process of review and reconstruction of their aims and approach. This perspective owes much, of course, to the way that literature works:

> Characters in stories are said to be compelling by virtue of our capacity for "identification" or because in their ensemble they represent the cast

of characters that we, the readers, carry unconsciously within us. (Bruner, 1986, p. 4)

We shall seek to offer other teachers convincing accounts of the *process* of change, viewed 'not through an omniscient eye . . . but through the filter of the consciousness of protagonists in the story' (ibid.). In drawing on the tradition of biography in educational research, we are exploring our own version of what Stake (1987) calls 'an evolutionary view' of staff development.

There is another strength of the biographical approach that I have not so far mentioned. The biographical method is, as Grumet (1981, p. 110) says, 'a process of restitution' that returns experience 'to the person who lived it'. To focus on the individual teacher requires an interesting modification of a traditional perspective (see Aspinwall, 1985, p. 67): the education system is dominated by two powerful hierarchies, the hierarchy of status and the hierarchy of knowledge production, and the classroom teacher is often at the bottom of both hierarchies. The biographical approach, therefore, helps the teacher to feel some sense of individual power-through-understanding at the centre of the action.

This focus on the individual is also important because individualism in teaching has tended to be associated with privacy (see Anderson and Snyder, 1982), and privacy can, of course, be a cover for conservatism. Our dealings with pupils reveal how difficult we find it, despite our speech-day rhetoric of 'helping each pupil develop his or her potential to the full', to honour individuality, except in the context of competitiveness. We have, as Linda McNeil points out, a remarkable commitment to 'teaching to sameness' and to dealing with individuals by categorizing them. When teachers talk about differences between pupils they tend to comment on 'girls' and 'boys'; they recall subsets of pupils who cannot read, who are slow, who have trouble writing. Pupils, on the other hand, talk about how the curriculum seems not to relate to them *personally*. McNeil (1987) suggests an important difference between a 'collective' where people work productively together because they recognize each individual's distinctive potential, and 'conformist groups' where members are treated as though they were a uniform body:

> Students rarely see themselves as part of a collective group . . . [when teachers] did attend to student differences, it was not to the kind of differences which students felt important to them as individuals . . . instead, the differences which teachers paid attention to tended to be those which were behavioural and procedural . . . which arose within and because of the instructional context rather than those that were brought to it. (p. 106)

Similarly, I would argue that we need to give attention to the behaviours and attitudes that teachers as individuals and as members of 'collectives', bring to the context of innovation. Teachers need to understand the structure of their own and their colleagues' and pupils' readiness for change and the basis of their own, and others', resistance to it.

To focus on the basis of the individual's commitment, values and talents is a way of strengthening the bonds that keep a working group together in the task of effecting change. In a working group that accepts the task of change, there must be a foundation of shared concern and shared sense of purpose. As Ionesco said, 'dreams and anguish bring us together' (quoted by Pratt, 1987). But within such a group each individual must, in my view, be there because he or she has a grasp of the basis of his or her own commitment that has deeper roots than the more obvious and possibly more superficial commonalities within the group. The group spirit may, through the sense of obligation and loyalty that it generates, keep the individuals going when the task of change proves difficult, but motivation must also derive from the individual's growing sense of personal understanding and control.

As Bruner (1986, pp. 13–14) said, the teacher facing change needs simultaneously to construct two landscapes, the landscape of consciousness, which is essentially about personal meanings, and the landscape of action, where some corporate sense of the political struggles needed to bring about change can be a source of strength. What I am proposing is that we help teachers with the task of constructing their own landscapes of consciousness.

In this chapter, I have proposed a particular view of 'the ownership of change'. I see it as bringing about a motivation towards change that is personally founded, and I see it as being about meaning that is explored in relation to the self as well as in relation to the professional context. Professional learning is, I think, more likely to be powerful in its engagement with fundamental issues in education if teachers have constructed their own narrative of the need for change. This view of the situation requires access to conceptions of critical theory as a basis for professional learning and recognizes that in situations where routinization and the reproduction of sameness are prevalent, practitioners need help in getting in touch with the values that drive their actions as teachers. A comment by Berlak (1985, p. 2) is apposite:

> People are liberated to the extent that they are, at the same time, increasingly free to choose from a range of alternative perspectives of themselves and their social worlds. This freedom of choice requires the ability to see one's own views of what is good or right, possible or impossible, true or false, as problematic, socially constructed [and] subject to social and political influence. (quoted in Smyth, 1987b, p. 23)

And, as Smyth says, if teachers can achieve and sustain such a perspective, they may play a more powerful role in the curriculum battles that are now being played out.

Appendix: Extracts from three science teachers' narratives of the growth of their acknowledgement of the need for change

Three teachers were involved as members of the university-based development team in a project that explored new teaching and learning strategies in science through the development of biotechnological content. All three had a one-day-a-week release in the first term of the project: teacher A then had a one-term secondment, teacher B a two-term secondment and teacher C a three-term secondment to continue on the project. The interviews from which these narratives were constructed took place towards the end of the first term's involvement.

Teacher A

I was doing research before I went into teaching, bench work mainly, pretty repetitive bench work and I got into this kind of rut working on this research, very isolated. I went straight into it. I never really questioned the whole momentum. I was on a sort of conveyor belt really. So I got out of that and into teaching. Now my teacher training more or less taught me basic strategies of control. What they were saying to me was that without these skills there won't be enough order for you to get the subject across. But it just didn't work in my first school. I went in with a mixture of rules of thumb that I'd got from the teacher training, plus my own visions, and it was just inappropriate. It just wore me down. I got to the point where I realized that there had to be a much deeper understanding of the relationship between me and the kids. I was burning up so much energy and seeing so little happiness and satisfaction and well-being amongst the kids.

A lot of my lessons would be very loud. I had this notion of a graded reprimand, so I'd start off with a fairly quiet reprimand, but it wasn't particularly friendly, and that would quickly escalate into me actually shouting at the kid and it would put all the other kids on edge: it would make them all defensive and it would very quickly create a sort of polarization of me against them. There had to be another way of operating. I guess that started to dawn on me.

One of the things that happened was I realized that I actually liked kids. Just that simple. I'd been so bound up in the mechanics of teaching that I'd not really had the leisure to reflect on why I had gone into something which I thought was less isolating. I realized that if I operated within the same framework that I had done before I was going to be just as isolated, and the realization that I actually liked kids made me want to explore that relationship and find teaching strategies that would support that relationship. I started to experiment a bit – doing more active work on environmental issues, me working with them, them working with me, having to team up with one another physically over jobs like erecting a fence.

And so from having been teacher as controller, I went to the other extreme, teacher as facilitator role. It helped me quite a lot with individuals, but I found it didn't help me with the group situation much. It was as though I was relating to the group as fragments. The group obviously had a sense of insecurity in the school as a whole: they were shifting from one lesson to another, from one style to another. I was trying to negotiate with the kids outside of any framework for negotiation and I was trying to throw the existing mode of control out of the window, and nobody could cope with that.

I think I was probably trying to move towards a relationship with the kids where I wasn't dominating them – some sort of relationship where we were cooperating in finding out something. But it was complicated. I didn't know a lot about it and I didn't understand very much about me. I just knew that I had previously disregarded things about me and what I'd done for a living that had led to trouble, and so I stuck with this new approach.

I suppose what I was beginning to feel was that as an individual I'd been absolutely swamped by all the pressures that the education system had put on me. I couldn't take it any more. I realized that it was leading me up blind alleys and I felt that I didn't want to lead kids up the same blind alley. In other words I was looking for ways to get involved in teaching science with kids and yet not at the same time destroy their autonomy. The thread had to be that we could explore scientific ideas, but it had to be in a framework where it wasn't simply me telling them. There had to be a possibility of them developing autonomously – not just as scientists but as people, and I felt that if that didn't happen I was doing them a profound disservice really.

Science for me has now come to mean a way of looking at the world which has got practical usefulness. You've got to look at it in terms of the whole planet and the way science is used in our society and all the consequences of it – right? Now how do you convey that to kids? We live in a society, it seems to me, where God and religion have just been replaced by the paradigm of science and technology. For me, that's incredibly dangerous, because you're simply taking one defunct ideology and slapping another in there. So how do I translate that into practical teaching approaches to kids? Well, try and extract general principles I suppose, like autonomy, and then translate that into practical strategies. Problem solving perhaps. I'm not going to stand at the front and say "This is the way to do it." Instead, I'll maybe try and present a secure framework – I've learnt that you've got to have a secure framework – but within that framework have sufficient open-endedness to allow some sort of exploration.

The notion of what I'm about has changed. I've stopped shifting from one paradigm to another – being authoritarian and then being non-authoritarian – just reacting against the previous image. I think I've now reached the point where I feel secure enough to be prepared to constantly reassess and re-evaluate what I'm doing. I've not got a fixed set of models that I'm sure will work, that I'm always going to stick to. I'm flexible – that's one of the main things I've learned.

Teacher B

I started my present school thirteen years ago – and I'm still there! I didn't go straight from teacher training to teach. I went to work as a research technician for two years, but I decided I really wasn't getting anywhere. I started as a physics teacher, but within two years I moved into biology and was immediately given the responsibility for the department. My first year was exceptionally difficult. I was given mainly bottom classes. It was around the time when the school leaving age was being raised to 16 and a lot of kids deeply resented being in school.

I learned very early on in teacher training that when you get into difficulties the very worst thing you can do is to try to emulate the science teacher who'd taught you in school.

I started off feeling that I was trying to make information attractive – information was the all important thing – and involving children in the activity; this was the other key. And I think that stayed with me for a long time until I began to have a number of misgivings without quite knowing what those misgivings were. I wanted to get over certain skills and certain information but at the same time I also felt that good teaching was busy children and busy children were thinking children. There was something there that didn't quite fit and I think part of that unease has only begun to unravel itself in this last term when I've had the chance to think more about things.

My unease reached a stage where I felt that something had got to be done about that – we'd got to analyse the way children think. At best I was reaching a few pupils for whom I would say science had succeeded – most of those were very able and going on to higher education. For a very large number of children, the very best I was achieving was a sort of benign tolerance of what they'd gone through in science. It wasn't something that was going to stay with them. At worst there was a clear antagonism. They weren't enjoying it – it was going to be of no use at all in later life and as far as making them scientifically competent in the modern world, it certainly wasn't achieving that. In that sense it was failing and I had a gut feeling that something needed changing. But quite frankly I didn't know what.

If things are not going well, there is a natural inclination to try to make your activities more teacher directed. I would sweat blood. I'd try to become the best showman in the world, try to entertain the children, but in the end I would assess pupils' performance and it was often very poor and I was very disturbed by it. I discovered that what I was doing was to transfer my assessment marks to a piece of paper and as soon as they became a set of numbers, I would play with them. I would draw normal distributions and it was just a big get out! You feel very safe as soon as you play with numbers but you lose sight of the pupils.

One of my strengths is that I'm quite a creative person – I can 'think' activity for children. If I look back on some of the things I created I think they were embryonic problem-solving tasks. So it was evolutionary – I started in a crude sort of way, almost unconsciously, and since I've been on the project I've recognized what it was that I was trying to do.

In the school I went to as a pupil I found the experience up to sixth form level dire in the extreme. It was unproductive. I went into the sixth form on the point of failing educationally. I just scraped in, did three sciences and loved every minute of it! To me it was the acquisition of information about the nature of the universe and everything to do with it that made a good scientist – with the associated skills. And still at university I thought it was about soaking up information. I don't think it even began to enter my head that solving problems had any real value. Most experiments that we had to carry out were not experiments – they were what I would recognize now as demonstrations.

Quite early on in the project, when we were coming in just one day a week and we started to trial the very first approaches in my school, a number of things occurred that really convinced me that I was at last on the right road. Firstly, I think the children were enjoying it. They were smiling more than they normally smile, and they were talking about science. They were much more engaged than they had been before. Secondly, there was a continuity from one lesson to another, they seemed to remember the things that had gone on in earlier lessons – for many of the less able children that was something that had not normally happened. For the first time I actually got them to talk rather than just write up an experiment – they talked in an open forum for the first time and listening to them questioning each other about each other's projects and seeing this ownership of their project, for the first time I began to realize that children – these children – had begun to understand at a level that was far deeper than I think I'd achieved before.

I'm having to change my mind quite a lot about fundamental things, but the principle is there that children don't just see science as something that they learn at school: they must see that it has a context and within that context there is responsibility. That was my starting point. Beyond that I began to think that if you try to teach responsibility, you become involved with the education of caring, and that is a fundamental tenet for me. The fact that I hadn't got it right in my lessons doesn't change that tenet – caring must lie somewhere at the heart of what I'm trying to do.

I think more than anything this new style of teaching is frighteningly involved, and I don't know whether, to be frank, I could sustain it on a regular basis. It challenges what I would normally do in the classroom. There is always a feeling, and it's something I've heard many teachers say, that as a teacher you've got to "teach": it's about getting up and doing something yourself. You feel this responsibility to somehow "do it". What is required is the confidence, once you've created an activity, to let it run.

Teacher C

I didn't do any teacher training. I sneaked in through the back door really. When I left school, I'd done 'A' level physics, chemistry and maths. But I was a bit of a rebellious pupil, and I was just fed up with studying. I wanted a job and I went into insurance – my maths background seemed to suit that. And I learned very quickly that it was deadly boring working in an office with about fifty other people about the same age as me. So I did some tuition in my second year of work, just a few Saturday mornings helping a youngster with some maths and I enjoyed doing it, so I thought "I know, I'll teach". But then, of course, I had to go on to further education. I lived in London, so I applied locally and went to a Poly to do an external degree. Biology had always been my favourite subject at school, but I'd dropped it at 'A' level, so I decided biology for me – and I wanted to teach.

I used to be able to do biology exams in school without any revision whatsoever. I just used to sit and listen to the teachers talking about it and it used to go in and I never had to think about it again. It was very old-fashioned stuff. It was the only way we were taught. . . . At the Poly it was an incredibly old-fashioned style of teaching as well. I just accepted it.

I started teaching at a comprehensive in 1973. I had had no previous experience at all of teaching anybody other than on an individual basis. The first class I ever took was a fifth year CSE group. I'd been told by the Head of Biology that if I had any problems at all just sling them out and he'd deal with them, so I went in fairly confident – I was innocent of what could happen. The lesson started off OK, but one lad played me up fairly early on, so bearing in mind what the Head of Biology had said, I just slung him straight out. What I hadn't realised was that this particular lad was on his final warning – if he misbehaved once more in anybody's lesson he would be expelled. That made my reputation with the kids – you know – OUT and he was never seen again! Basically I found the kids incredibly easy to get on with and I had no discipline problems at all. I just felt at home with them because they were the sort of kids I'd grown up with, and I hadn't been out of school myself that long.

But I was never quite sure what the kids were taking in. I suppose I didn't have the experience to say "Stop; let's talk about it." I just let it continue and I used to find that very unsettling – you know – *are* they actually taking it in? But the exams came up and they seemed to be doing all right, so I thought it must be working and I didn't look at it any closer than that! If things seem to be going OK, I tend to look at them rather superficially and allow them to carry on. It's only when things go wrong I start looking at them.

Then I moved up here and things went quite well for a while but I found that I was beginning to get very frustrated with teaching. I found that some kids were not responding to my approach as well as they used to, but some were, and I used to find that in the end, I was getting to know those few very well and they'd get to know me very well, but there were a number within a class that I was not communicating with. They didn't seem to want to, and it was beginning to rattle me. It was either going over their heads or they just weren't switching on to my lessons. I wasn't getting through to them at all and I used to try to talk to some of them about it but they just didn't want to know.

I felt I was still teaching in an interesting way, trying to get something from them, but it was getting less and less effective and even areas of work that I'd introduced several years ago that had been a tremendous success when I first started, even they were failing, and I was beginning to think "Well, I'm going to have to change this." And I couldn't understand why if I was doing the same thing, using the same material that was successful seven years ago, why it wasn't successful now. That had really begun to bug me.

I found that I was having to put more pressure on the pupils to keep them in line whereas before I never had to bother about discipline. Something was definitely going adrift somewhere and I think it was about that point that I started coming here on the Fridays for the biotechnology project. Actually, the adviser who told me about the project did say that it would involve my being filmed teaching: this sounded interesting but it worried me a bit. I'd never had anybody in my lessons at any time in my entire teaching career, so to go straight to actually having a camera operating was a giant step, but I thought, "I'll tackle that one when I come to it." That was the only thing that worried me about it. I also wasn't quite sure what biotechnology was when he first mentioned it. From a purely selfish point of view it has been absolutely superb for me, because it's the first time I've actually been able to sit down and think about what I'm actually doing in teaching. I've gone through basically ignorant of the philosophies behind what I was actually trying to do. I've not really sat down myself and thought "Why am I teaching this particular area – why am I using that approach?" I just played it by ear. I just worked on instinct most of the time.

There obviously had been problems building up at school for which I was blaming various things, but to actually sit down with other people who obviously were thinking far more about what they were doing while they were doing it than I tend to – that was great! I dream about things and daydream. I tend to be a quiet person anyway, and this term has really changed that for me. I feel far more able to think something out and verbalize it to other people and argue a point through. It's enabled me to focus far more on what possibly has been going wrong in my teaching.

Now, after this term of secondment, I'm going to be able to think about what I'm trying to do, what approaches can be used, and certainly when I went back into school to trial the materials, I definitely felt really comfortable and happy again with teaching – the first time for quite some time. I was asking more from the kids and asking them to, in a sense, control their own destiny in the lesson, but in doing that it actually built communication between myself and the kids. They felt I was coming round to help them with the problem *I'd* given them, which they might feel wasn't theirs. The communication came back with a rush and I suddenly realised why I enjoy teaching and all the old enjoyment, all the old feelings and pleasures were there again.

Note

The interviews referred to in this chapter are reproduced in full as part of the *Biotechnology in Secondary Schools Project* published by the Division of Education, University of Sheffield (1987), and directed by Jenny Henderson, with assistance from Stephen Knutton.

9 Understanding the World of the Classroom: the Importance of a Research Perspective

Art is a metaphor that helps us and the teachers we work with build a shared understanding of the problems of improving professional understanding and practice. As Stenhouse (1984b, p. 70) said, to say that teaching is an art reminds us that teachers, like artists, must work hard to impove their practice: think for instance of a quartet rehearsing together a composition that they had not played before, or of a ballet dancer working at a particular movement again and again in order to maximize technical control and expressiveness. Another important route to the improvement of one's art as a teacher is the disciplined monitoring of one's own practice. And the exciting thing about art and, by analogy, teaching, is that the improvement of the art is achieved through the exercise of the art (Stenhouse, 1980b, p. 41). You become a better poet or painter by critically examining the work that you produce, provided that you constantly criticize your aspirations and believe that what you struggle to understand or to communicate through your art is worthwhile and therefore worth the effort of critical reflection. Teachers, like artists, can learn from and through the reflective study of their everyday activity. For the moment, let us call this critical habit of enquiry into practice 'research'.

One problem with using the word 'research' is that the right to produce worthwhile knowledge through research has traditionally been claimed by members of an academic elite. Traditionally, research has been located in universities, not in schools, and the language of research reportage often shows little concern for the theoretical literacy of teachers. In short, a concern to communicate with practitioners has not, until fairly recently, characterized the work of the university-based researcher.

Another problem relates to the dominance of quantitative research methodologies: the legacy has been difficult to dispel despite increasing publicity for, and confidence in, qualitative approaches. In quantitative research, findings tend to be expressed as generalizations, and generalizations do not help the individual teacher to decide what action to take in the particular context of his or her own setting. As Cronbach (1975, p. 125) suggests: 'When we give proper weight to local conditions, any generalization is a working hypothesis, not a conclusion.' The logic of this position is that the results of research need testing in local conditions or, to put it another way, the proper response from teachers to the research carried out by others is to replicate the research in the particularity of their own classrooms: 'using' research means, therefore, 'doing' research (Stenhouse, 1979). But, of course, research has not been seen as part of the teacher's professional responsibility; nor, therefore, has it featured prominently in courses of initial teacher education.

I would go further than Cronbach and suggest that what research can best offer teachers is, first, hypotheses that may contribute an agenda for teacher research and, secondly, cases that provide a basis for judgement about the action that individual teachers might take in their own settings:

> Characteristically, they [teachers] may be thought of as responsible not for formulating policy across cases . . . but for the conduct of their own cases familiar to them. Their need is to apply knowledge to specific and individual situations. (Stenhouse, 1984a, p. 264)

Case studies offer evidence of the effects of action in other settings and thereby alert teachers to factors that may significantly affect the outcomes of particular courses of action in their own setting. They also assist teachers with the development of critical judgement by 'extending vicariously their experience of schools or classrooms' – and critical judgement is crucial to the task of improving the quality of teaching and learning.

But first something needs to be said about the pay-off for teachers involving themselves in school-based or classroom-based research. First, by helping teachers to become competent critics and interpreters of research and by giving them some grounding in research skills, one is contributing to what I would say is a necessary demystification of research within the educational system. Secondly, research offers a way of marking out a path of professional development: it offers a way of structuring a familiar situation that allows the teacher to explore it in depth, to gain new insights, to set new goals, and to achieve new levels of competence and confidence. In this way, the teacher has a sense of the professional progress that he or she is making. Thirdly, research liberates curiosity and generates intellectual excitement – and now more than at any time the teaching profession needs intellectual excitement. Research, I would claim, is a defence against the sameness of teaching. As Schon (1983, p. 69) suggests:

> A professional practitioner is a specialist who encounters certain types of situation again and again . . . [but] many practitioners, locked into a view of themselves as technical experts, find nothing in the world of practice to occasion reflection. They have become too skilful at techniques of selective inattention, junk categories, and situational control, techniques which they use to preserve the constancy of their knowledge-in-practice.

Teaching is vulnerable to the flattening effect of habit, and research can help teachers see behind what is taken for granted in everyday practice. Habit is seductive: it is soothing and compulsive. I am suggesting, however, that good teaching is essentially experimental, and experiment entails rescuing at least part of one's work from the predictability of routine. But 'experiment', like 're-search', is an uncomfortable word for many teachers – and for many parents. Typically, the response of parents to the idea of classroom 'experiment' is that they don't want their children treated as 'guinea-pigs'. Now the interesting thing about classroom research undertaken by teachers is that the research act must be educationally justifiable: at no time can research curiosities subvert educational principles. Indeed, one could argue that it is the child in the everyday world of the classroom, where the pattern of teaching and learning remains unexamined, that is at risk because he or she is subject to constant unmonitored and unreflected-on action. *Not* to examine one's practice is irre-sponsible: to regard teaching as an experiment and to monitor one's perfor-mance is a responsible professional act (see Stenhouse, 1980b).

Problems of initiating teacher research

What of the research that teachers might undertake, not as a way of testing other people's research findings but as a response to the dilemmas, anxieties and aspirations they experience in their own schools and classrooms? The general focus for such enquiry may be determined by an individual teacher, a group of teachers, or by a school staff as a whole, but the difficult step is to *frame* a particular problem in ways that allow it to be opened up and explored. To get a research grip on a problem often requires that teachers learn to see 'ordinary' events and interactions with new eyes, for significances become obscured by the familiarity of the everyday context. The everyday eyes of teachers have two weaknesses. First, because of the dominance of habit and routine, teachers are only selectively attentive to the phenomena of their classrooms. In a sense they are constantly reconstructing the world they are familiar with in order to maintain regularities and routines. Secondly, because of their busyness, their eyes tend only to transcribe the surface realities of classroom interaction. The aim in teacher research is for the teacher to attain the eyes of the artist, for it is art that teaches the sensitivity of being attentive to significances that normally remain uncelebrated. As Seifert (1983, p. 56) has said:

> In the outlines of the things on which I look
> I paint what the eye does not see.
> And that is art.

A precondition of teacher research may well be that the teacher has tem-porarily to become a stranger in his or her own classroom (see Greene, 1973). Teachers must abandon their habitual way of perceiving their world in order to be receptive to its problematics. They must acquire eyes that are capable of perceiving the seeds of a worthwhile problem and then they must frame that problem, gather data, derive explanations and test those explanations. Here the art/science dichotomy is useful, for one might claim that art is a way of representing reality and science is a way of explaining the same reality (Read, 1958). Both are central aspects of classroom-based research.

Our experience of working with groups of novitiate teacher researchers suggests that it is important to sanction a period of reconaissance so that a broad research concern can be structured as a tighter research question. Teachers need to be tolerant of the ambiguity of the situation – and patient. A useful discipline is to be sensitive to surprise. There will often be occasions during a school week when the predicted flow of events in the classroom is broken. The flow of experience is arrested, but usually the teacher rapidly restructures his or her view of the situation, reviews alternative courses of action, selects what appears to be the best at the moment, and acts. In these moments of surprise, the learning potential is high but is often lost because routine quickly flows back to fill the vacuum that surprise has temporarily created. As soon as things get back on course, the structure of the situation that created the hiatus and caused surprise is lost to the teacher's consciousness. For the teacher who is trying to sharpen a research focus these moments are rich, but it is not easy when one is engaged in the relentless pressure of the classroom to take time off to record the structure of the event at the time. Some teacher researchers have used the simple device of keeping a notebook on the desk in which they jot down a few key words that will help them to recreate the situation at the moment when it impinged on their consciousness. One teacher we worked with, for example, had identified 'children's management of the hidden curriculum' as a broad research interest. During his period of reconaissance, when he was intent on identifying lines of worthwhile enquiry, he managed to jot down, during lessons, scraps of dialogue or observations that he registered at the time as of interest and that he knew he would have forgotten by the end of the day. His jottings enabled him to reconstruct the event or situation at leisure and to reflect on it. Here is one example of a 'jotting', filled out a little to make it comprehensible to present readers:

> Individual Work Cards. There's an initial rush to complete one card – the minimum requirement. When this is completed, though another card is often collected, intensive work ceases, and chatting, with some desultory work, is the norm. Talk is voluntarily kept at a quiet level – so that the teacher's attention is not drawn to what is happening?

Observations such as this were a powerful means of mapping the territory of the teacher's concerns. He went on building up his data base, reflecting on it and sharpening his understanding of the dimensions of the problem until he was able to frame a research task that was manageable given the constraints of practitioner research (see Hull *et al.*, 1985).

Another way of seeing through the familiar during this period of research reconaissance is for teachers to video-tape or audio-tape samples of their everyday teaching. In this way, something of the unseen, or forgotten, complexity of the situation is captured, so that teachers can reflect on it at leisure and with the eyes of the observer rather than the actor. Such records are partial but none the less powerful:

Spent four hours tonight listening to tapes from today's lessons. My voice was a sort of heartless monotone most of the time; there were at least three instances of my being unnecessarily hard on kids . . . there were four cases of children saying something interesting which I had not followed up at the time – I'm sure I didn't even hear them during the lesson. I was so busy chanting my own little pearls of wisdom . . . I realise that I derive considerable security from having kids as a captive audience. (A teacher reflecting on the task of monitoring her teaching: from Rudduck, 1979, p. 45)

While most supporters of classroom-based teacher research agree that the most profitable starting points are specific problems or questions, there is a tendency to overestimate the ease with which the 'real' problem that often lies beneath the surface definition can be teased out. A period of responsive observation can be useful: curiosity or concern broadly directs the initial observation; the preliminary evidence focuses reflection, and reflection enables the teacher researcher to refine understanding, move towards the articulation of a research question that is rooted in the reality of a particular setting, and thence to an appropriate research design.

Community and status in teacher research

In the world of the arts, form is what makes possible a dialogue between the sensitivity of the individual artist and the collective sensitivity of the community that determines what counts as art. The zoo-keeper (see Becker, 1982) who wanted to call the elephant he tended a 'work of art' was not in touch with the thinking of the guardians of standards in the world of art which he aspired to join, nor was he in a position to influence the judgement of that community. Duchamp (1962), however, claiming that a public urinal – a 'ready-made' – could be presented as a work of art was at least allowed to engage in a debate that was capable of extending the boundary of the acceptable. He remarked, somewhat cynically, 'I threw the bottle rack and the urinal into their faces as a challenge and now they admire them for their aesthetic beauty.'

I do not want to press the analogy with the world of educational research too closely, but the story serves to cue us in to some of the issues. Practitioner researchers, rather like the zoo-keeper, are in an ambiguous position in terms of their place in the research community and the status of the research that they produce. As I suggested earlier, 'academic' researchers dominate thinking and practice in educational research; they are the ones who are licensed to challenge the conventions, and they have easy access to, and control over, the channels of research communication. Moreover, most schools, even if they chose to, could not afford to stock educational research journals in their school libraries, and teachers' centres tend not to give a high priority to subscriptions to academic research journals. Teachers are, then, by and large, cut off from access to research reportage except when the popular educational press offers summary accounts or when a report becomes a 'bestseller'. If teachers have such little access to reported research it is difficult for them (unless, of course, they are on a research-based higher degree course) to relate their enquiries to other work in the field, and to convert the fruits of their enquiries into mainstream educational research knowledge.

What, then, is the status and future of teacher research? Is it enough that it feeds only individual or local understanding and insight? If we take as a definition (Stenhouse, 1984c, p. 77) research as systematic enquiry made public, then the enquiries that teachers undertake in their own settings have to become accessible to public critique, or we have to deny those activities the status of research. In thinking about these issues, we have to take into account the fact that training in research is not conventionally on the agenda of initial teacher education courses. Moreover, practitioners, unlike academic staff in universities, do not have research as part of their contract and there is no specific time allowance to support the research enterprise. Given such constraints, is it reasonable to withdraw the challenge in the title, teacher-as-researcher, and to accept the gentler phrase of Schon – the 'reflective' practitioner'? But if we do so, we may lose one important potential of the movement – the opening up of the established research tradition and the democratization of the research community.

10 Partnerships for Building Understanding

Professional development is about the capacity of a teacher to remain curious about the classroom; to identify significant concerns in the process of teaching and learning; to value and seek dialogue with experienced colleagues as support in the analysis of situations; and to adjust patterns of classroom action in the light of new understandings. As Joyce and Clift (1984, p. 8) point out: 'It is unthinkable that professional skill could be sustained on anything but a growing foundation of knowledge.' If they are right, and I believe they are, then we must try to instil a habit of curiosity in student teachers and make sure that opportunities are provided, in the relentless busyness of classroom teaching, that will allow experienced teachers to continue to learn.

'Partnership supervision' can meet such purposes. It rests on the straightforward assumption that the understandings implicit in teachers' intuitiveness and experience can be transformed into educational knowledge through critical reflection on practice and focused dialogue. Partnership supervision can be used during the initial training of teachers and as a basis for in-service activity. In each setting, it provides a framework in which the school teacher and an outsider, such as a university lecturer or adviser, work together to analyse and learn from the evidence of the teacher's classroom. It operates within principles of naturalistic enquiry and the process can be assisted by the teacher's openness to accounts of classroom practice derived from studies undertaken in other classrooms.

Why the need for partnership? The structures of schooling, despite efforts at establishing open classrooms and team teaching, still press towards the isolation of teachers. Moreover, the culture of many school common rooms is not one that legitimizes serious discussion of classroom events and interactions. In addition, the agenda for meetings of the whole staff of a school, or of teachers within a subject department, tend to support the discussion of administrative matters rather than fundamental values that underpin practice. Partnership supervision, which supports dialogue between a teacher and an outsider, re-establishes the importance of focused professional dialogue.

The use of an outsider as partner is not necessarily a disadvantage. An outsider is in a good position to help experienced teachers to loosen the hold of habit. Immersion in the world of routine practice can tend, over time, to reduce the capacity of the practitioner both to contemplate alternative courses of action and to continue to gain insight from everyday events. As insight goes, so some of the intellectual excitement of teaching goes too. A new perspective is needed that can bring back freshness of vision. The outsider can help the teacher to see the classroom differently and can offer alternative ways of giving meaning to what is happening. Thus, partnership supervision helps experienced teachers to achieve a new understanding of everyday classroom events and interactions. Moreover, it operates in such a way that teachers will feel that their control of the situation is heightened and not threatened by their association with an 'expert' outsider.

As far as students on initial training courses are concerned, partnership supervision can help them to value from the start of their career the insight and confidence that professional dialogue can yield. It can help students see what experienced 'others' may have to offer, even though these 'others' come from worlds that teachers often reject as academically or bureaucratically irrelevant. It can also help build the kind of understanding-in-context that will enable new teachers to develop and articulate their own theories of what happens in classrooms. Such things are, I think, the foundation of the teacher's professional identity and sense of power within the system.

Partnership supervision: Principles of procedure

Partnership supervision is a version of the model of clinical supervision (see Goldhammer, 1969; Cogan, 1973) that has been widely used in Canada and the USA, but which, according to Smyth (1985), has had a chequered history. It has been criticized as unworkable in schools, but such criticisms may well be the product not only of an over-rigid interpretation of the code of practice recommended but also of the generally distancing associations of the word 'clinical': we chose to drop it – but that leaves the word 'supervision', which also has its problems! As Smyth (1985, p. 5) says, it is not surprising that teachers come to regard supervisory practices with a jaundiced eye, and he quotes Withall and Wood (1979, p. 55):

> [Supervision] connotes a situation that is unpleasant, poses psychological threat and typically culminates in unrewarding consequences. . . . Supervisors have tended to project an image of superiority and omniscience in identifying the strengths and weaknesses of a teacher's performance and in offering advice concerning how to improve future performance.

However, despite the negative associations of the word 'supervision', we have retained it in the hope that people who are in traditional authority-linked supervisory roles might use our accounts of partnership supervision to rethink the basis of their relationship with both student teachers and experienced teachers.

In practice, partnership supervision falls into three stages of activity that together form a cycle:

(a) Pre-observation discussion, where one partner proposes a focus for observation and where the proposal is discussed and clarified.
(b) The period of observation of teaching.
(c) Post-observation discussion, where the observer's field notes are discussed in relation to the agreed focus.

Ideally, there would be a gap between the first and second cycles to allow time for reflection and consequent adjustment of the focus but, in practice, stage (c) of cycle 1 and stage (a) of cycle 2 are sometimes handled in the same meeting.

We have tried out partnership supervision in both pre-service and in-service settings: in the context of practice teaching where the partnership engages a student teacher and a supervisory tutor; and in the context of in-service work where a teacher and an outsider (in our case, university lecturers) form a partnership. To help define the relationship between the partners in each setting we relied on a formal contract derived from the clinical supervision model. The contract was drawn up to contain the authority of the partner who was likely to be perceived as more powerful by virtue of his or her institutional position. The most distinctive item in the contract is that the focus for the observation is always determined by the partner whose teaching is being observed and not, as in traditional supervisory relationships, by the partner whose status and/or more extensive experience tends to lead him or her to call the tune. The terms of the contract we used were simple and straightforward:

1. The partner whose teaching will be observed proposes a focus for observation by nominating one or more topics or problems that he or she would like to have feedback on. The focus is discussed and clarified until both partners feel that they have arrived at a shared understanding.
2. The partners consider what kind of evidence would illuminate the agreed focus and, given the constraints of the situation, how best the evidence might be gathered.
3. The observing partner agrees to shape his or her observation to the agreed focus.
4. The observing partner agrees to discipline the content of his or her post-observation feedback by accepting a strict principle of relevance as defined by the focus.

Teaching partners tend to identify practical problems as a focus for observation and observers tend to make field notes that provide a descriptive account of relevant classroom episodes. Smyth (1985) argues that supervisory procedures that are confined to the describing and correcting of problems within teaching are of limited potential, but I think he underestimates the significance of such a process. In our experience, neither new teachers nor established teachers find it easy to get a critical grip on the values and structures that are shaping practice and holding convention in place. If partnership supervision, by focusing sympathetically on immediate problems, encourages teachers to reflect on practice and to speculate about the possibilities for change, then we must surely see this as a step in the right direction. Indeed, to move from such a position to one that allows a more fundamental critique of the teacher's framework of action may require more than a supervisory relationship can in fact offer. It may require opportunities for reading and debate that help teachers to reach behind and beyond the immediately apparent dilemmas of daily practice so that they can understand the force and interplay of historical, political and social pressures as well as see more clearly how to 'act to change existing power relationships that have become frozen and formalized and are no longer subject to question' (Smyth, 1985, p. 11). We may need, therefore, to look to the more sustained learning of a higher degree course for the development of such a critical perspective.

Partnership supervision in practice I: Pre-service[1]

In trying out partnership supervision with students on initial training, our concern was to try to establish a habit of reflection on practice and to help students appreciate the value of open dialogue grounded in the events of the classroom. In our exploratory study, we worked with four students who were following a one-year postgraduate course of teacher training for the primary (elementary) school. We joined them in the third and final terms of their training. By this time, they had already experienced the college's conventional approach to supervision in which a tutor can 'drop in' on a student teacher, sometimes without warning, to observe a lesson, note a variety of points – usually both strengths and weaknesses of performance – and report on the performance. Occasionally, if tutors have another student to visit and time is short, they might hand over a copy of their essentially judgemental written statement and depart after only the briefest of conversations. The four students who took part in the trial of partnership supervision were volunteers from a select group of students whom their tutors felt were pretty certain to pass on their final teaching practice. We did not feel that it was justifiable to work experimentally with students who were known to be borderline, lest the new style of supervision be blamed for any failure on their part to meet the required standard.

In our work with student teachers, three things surprised us. First, we found that the problems that students identified were often not ones that featured on the tutor's standard list of diagnoses. We realized the extent to which we, as supervisors, were routinely reconstructing classrooms in conventional, stereotypical images. We were not, in our busy, hit-and-run visits, taking the time to look at the distinctive or unique features of the situations our students were working in. This came home to us most forcibly when one student proposed that the difficulties she was experiencing might be related to her 'looking so young'. She asked her partnership supervisor to observe her interaction with the class, taking her appearance as a starting point. Her partner acknowledged that the novelty of the focus helped him to look afresh at the classroom.

A second surprise was that students seemed to be acquiring an eye for significant detail. We attributed this to the documentary style of field notes that the observer used to capture the events of the classroom for discussion. Supervisors quite often offer students written comments that consist mainly of their views of the strengths and weaknesses of the student's handling of a lesson. A typical sentence in such a report is as follows: 'You have a good working relationship with your group and your control was quiet and unobtrusive. . . keep up the good work' (Rudduck and Sigsworth, 1983, p. 15). In partnership supervision, the same tutor's notes took a very different form:

> Girl. Fair-haired. Dress – green top, green/white striped skirt.
> Is writing
> My tray is . . . wide
> Copies it – distracted by my presence. Intervenes with child measuring table length in milk mats. Picks up box of rods – goes to wall unit takes out tray – goes to teacher – takes tray back to rack – sits on floor – then does not measure – re-boxes cuisenaire rods, returns to table. (ibid., p. 15)

Presented with detailed evidence of classroom action and interaction, students came to appreciate the power of vivid detail as a basis for reflection and understanding and they were often ready to 'play back', in the post-observation discussion, vivid episodes that they had stored in their mind from other lessons and that they now wanted to draw on as further evidence to support their emerging theories.

A third outcome was the readiness of students, hinted at in the last paragraph, to see theory and theorizing as something relevant to what goes on in classrooms. Analytic, research-based studies of education that students are encouraged to read while training and which are often criticized as irrelevant to the immediate demands of learning to teach, were now explicitly referred back to as students sought ways of thinking about the evidence of the classroom that would help them understand what was happening. In exploring this development, we speculated about the limitations of conventional teaching practice supervision where tutors tend to comment on a wide range of topics from their standard checklist, i.e. timing, pace, discipline, voice production, blackboard writing, lesson structure, strategies for encouraging participation, questioning technique, etc. The comments seldom cohere. An advantage of the partnership approach is that the agreed focus for observation unifies the observer's contributions, and the dynamic reality of the interplay between evidence and explanation helps the students to see what theory and theorizing are about.

Contrary to our initial expectations, the main problems in operating partnership supervision with student teachers lay not with the students, but with the tutors who had to struggle out of the straitjacket of their conventional supervisory ways. Some aspects of the approach presented a fundamental challenge to the assumptions on which tutors had been working: 'Normally, if you enter a student's classroom you sit down and *you* define what the situation is. You look at it through your own eyes – the eyes of somebody who has been in a lot of classrooms' (Rudduck and Sigsworth, 1985, p. 156). The responsibility of responding to issues that students identified and which were on the whole highly personalized and unpredictable was at first unnerving. One tempting but dysfunctional way of reducing the anxiety was to reformulate the student's idiosyncratic problems in terms of a familiar category, thus making it the tutor's problem rather than the student's. Tutors were also tempted to 'see' more than they were asked to see and they admitted to feeling guilty if they didn't 'tell' the student everything that they had noticed – again a legacy from past practice. Another legacy was the temptation to become prescriptive in the post-observation discussion when their task was, instead, to help students reflect on the evidence and arrive at their own interpretations and proposals for action. A problem of a different kind is presented by the contractual requirement to produce evidence for discussion. Tutors, as we saw above, are used to making judgements in their note books; sometimes they document events which support their judgements but rarely it seemed did the evidence of the classroom that they chose to record allow a student to appeal against the judgements. In partnership supervision, tutors were required to produce fuller accounts of events of the classroom, which were open to different interpretations, and they had to acquire some of the skills of the ethnographer.

Overall, we were heartened by our small-scale experiment. By fostering dialogue in a situation that minimizes the tutor's institutional power and instead emphasizes a colleague-like relationship, the student's developing sense of 'self as teacher' is nurtured. Moreover, the student begins to appreciate the value of professional dialogue, which helps him or her to reflect on and analyse the events and structures of particular classrooms.

The main problem of operating partnership supervision with student teachers was that of assessment: can the supervisor accept the responsibility of making an overall judgement of students' competence to teach without destroying the trust that characterizes the supervisory relationship? We think that this is possible but that it requires a substantial shift of perspective. Judgement, in partnership supervision, is based not only on the student's performance in the classroom, but also on his or her capacity to reflect on and analyse the events of the classroom in dialogue. In our in-service work, this problem did not exist.

Partnership supervision in practice II: In-service[2]

We also explored the potential of partnership supervision in in-service training. We worked with individual teachers in small and relatively isolated rural schools. The teachers rarely travelled to in-service events in teachers' centres in the cities and they welcomed the idea of professional contact with sympathetic outsiders who were prepared to visit them on their patch. Their professional experience so far had led them to classify visitors as either casual classroom tourists or as officials bent on inspection. Our colleagues tended to fall into the latter category. As one teacher made clear:

I imagined it was going to be a little like college and a tutor coming in and a final assessment for teaching practice – that sort of thing. The night before you came I sat there and I was a bit concerned about what I was going to do and what you were going to do and what we were going to talk about. (May and Sigsworth, 1982, p. 46)

On the whole, however, we were not so easily stereotyped. We were clearly not narrowly 'academic' because we had professed a readiness to spend time working in the classroom, but our credibility as critics of classroom practice was not so great as to be threatening.

We worked only with teachers who entered the partnership willingly: we were well aware what the likely effects of conscription could be. Teachers who are pressed into partnership might react with the defensive moves characteristic of students on conventionally supervised practice teaching. They might offer, for example, a spurious focus for observation or engineer events so as to render any real problems unobservable. Such defensive strategies might of course be legitimate in circumstances where it is against the teacher's real wishes to be involved, but they are unlikely to provide a foundation on which partnership supervision can be successfully developed. Our task was to build trust by demonstrating the seriousness of our claim to want to learn alongside the teachers in a non-exploitative fashion. The partnership supervision contract that we had used with students in initial training, as described earlier, suited our purpose well.

We noted that the teachers, even though they were experienced, still wanted to explore fairly concrete problems – in much the same way that students in pre-service training did. For instance, topics proposed included the non-participation of a few pupils in a drama lesson, the best use of space in a primary classroom, and so on. We were also aware that when working with experienced teachers, there is a greater pressure on the outsider to take part in the action rather than to gather data to assist the reflection. It is, of course, understandable if harassed teachers, finding another adult in the classroom, are tempted to use him or her as another pair of hands rather than as another pair of eyes. But in our view, the way of handling classroom problems that is generated through involvement in partnership supervision is likely to serve the teacher after the partnership is over, whereas the help that is given by a temporary teaching assistant usually ends with the departure of the assistant. In the primary classroom, however, the outsider may need to offer token participation in the activities in order to allay the curiosity of the children. Our outsiders found themselves tying knots, holding pieces of string for children to cut, and unjamming scissors.

In order to illustrate the way that the terms of the contract operate to serve the teacher and protect him or her from domination by the outsider, I will quote from the dialogue between a teacher and her partner: they are talking about the use of space in a classroom inhabited by twenty-six 5-year-old pupils. The observer had used his field notes to reconstruct various events that seemed to him to be shaped by the problem of pupils' movement about the room.

Having offered his reconstruction of events, his role was then to sustain the flow of reflection that the comments he offered had released:

> *Teacher.* I mean, really I suppose in some ways I'm not utilizing it to its best because originally that area taken up by the dolls' house was meant to be my sort of craft/paint area, which was the reason for the old carpet, because I had easels there so they could paint on the old carpet, and it didn't matter, and they were nearer the sink. But then that was a problem because it wasn't big enough for more than two, and then it was going to be a glueing area, then I realized I needed a place to put all my stuff for collage work. I think I really ought to do something about that area.
>
> *Outsider.* Yes, well, what's it possible to do? You need all that stuff.
>
> *Teacher.* The trolleys are another thing that – whether I move those and put them underneath the shelves on the carpet area or not . . .
>
> *Outsider.* I wondered about that. Do they all sit on the carpet for stories and things?
>
> *Teacher.* Yes, and some of them lean on the shelves.

Through the talk – at first almost pedestrian – the teacher was able to move towards her own solution to the problem of space and to think through what it was that had stopped her experimenting with the classroom layout. It seemed that the images of good teaching and of what a good classroom should look like, which had been instilled during her initial training course, were still so powerful that they had led her to maintain a pattern of practice that was in fact at odds with her own professional preferences and her immediate classroom needs:

> I suppose really the answer is, you know, to stop thinking about the way you've been trained, to stop thinking in "areas". When I was at college it was the late sixties/early seventies – it was very much the thing. You've got to have areas – you've got to have a Maths area, an activities area, and your quiet area. So, you know, it's very hard to get your mind off that.

A particular bonus of partnership with an outsider is the leverage he or she can offer to the teacher who faces the inertia of the past and has lost the energy to change. In this situation, the outsider, representing a different reference group from that of the lecturer-cum-judge of this teacher's student years, was able to support her in challenging the doctrine that had stifled her initiative.

Outsider partners, it seems, can also help teachers feel in closer touch with the world beyond their own classroom and school. But more than that, teachers who are professionally isolated have had no sure sense of their own quality as teachers. Regular appraisal will help with this when it is finally introduced in UK schools. In relation to the problems they encounter in their teaching it's easy to think, as one teacher we worked with put it, 'Perhaps it's me. When you hear [about] somebody else finding a problem then you think, "Well, I'm not so bad after all" ' (May and Sigsworth, 1982, p. 54). Partnership supervision can restore the teacher's confidence by helping him or her to see that the problem may lie in the complexities of the situation – in which, of course, the teacher is a part – and may not be a direct consequence of the teacher's shortcomings. Failure to understand the scene is easier to confront, it seems, than failure of performance.

The drawback to the approach is that for the outsider the time commitment is a major problem. The partnership should ideally be maintained over a reasonable series of meetings if the teacher is to risk entering into the spirit of the contract and face once again his or her own need to learn.

Partnership supervision, educational knowledge and the professional development of teachers

The convention whereby 'theory' and 'practice' have been separated and set up in opposition to each other has made it difficult to think straightforwardly about the ways in which 'knowledge' relates to the professional development of teachers (see Squirrell *et al.*, 1990). The production of respectable educational knowledge has been the responsibility of the university and in order to share this knowledge teachers have had to enter the world and the discourse of academia. Many 'academics' are themselves now challenging these constraints. Carr (1980), for instance, has criticized 'the dubious assumptions on which the . . . divide is based' and his claims are bold:

> There are no "educational phenomena" apart from the practices of those engaged in educational activities, no "educational problems" apart from those arising from these practices and no "educational theories" apart from those that structure and guide these practices. (Carr, 1982, p. 26)

The only task that educational theory can legitimately pursue, he continues, is 'to develop theories of educational practice that are intrinsically related to practitioners' own accounts of what they are doing' (ibid.). Such theories can help teachers to improve their practice by transforming the ways in which practice is experienced and understood; but this transformation depends on teachers' capacity for critical reflection. Partnership supervision, as I have tried to show, is a way of encouraging the spirit and practice of critical reflection.

Joyce and Clift (1984) take up the same issue from a slightly different perspective in their manifesto for reform in teacher education. They suggest that an important move for teachers 'is from a theoryless, totally pragmatic frame of reference to one where the quest for knowledge and the tasks of the workplace exist in a dynamic and compatible ambience'. Teachers 'function consistently as situational decision-makers' claims Bolster (1983, p. 302), and improvement in their understanding is tied up in their grasp of some of the constellations of events that seem important in their classrooms. Their judgement tends, however, not to be fully articulated, even as personal policy. There is a kind of parallel here with the lot of the student teacher: conventionally, the subculture of teacher training leads student teachers to place a higher value on practice teaching than on knowledge of educational research and theory, thus establishing a divide from the outset of their professional lives. And yet without some awareness of their right to criticize theory through practice and to use the critical perspectives offered by good research to understand their teaching, they are unlikely to move beyond a limited and ultimately disabling professionalism.

In our second exploration of partnership supervision with experienced teachers, the academics and practitioners were yoked together without the issues of knowledge-discovery and theory-building being clarified. Both partners seemed to accept, implicitly, that the aim was not to generate universal propositions about teaching and learning but rather to build a coherent explanation of why things happen as they do in one particular classroom (see Bolster, 1983). Understanding was rooted in the thick description of the field notes but it was often influenced by the wider perspectives that the outsider had access to. The energy that fuels the act of collaborative interpretation comes from the sparking of two perspectives. One is that of the *insider*, who has the intimate knowledge of the setting but whose responses come, in time, to be guided by habit. The second is that of the *outsider*, whose wares include ways of 'seeing' and thinking about the interaction of teaching and learning which he or she has developed through broad experience of classrooms and through critical reflection on different conceptual frameworks for analysing what goes on in classrooms.

Partnership supervision, like Bolster's idiographic model of research,

> provides an in-depth understanding of the complexity of a particular classroom . . . focuses on situated meanings . . . assumes multiple causalities of events . . . [and accepts that] unexpected contingencies [will] probably illuminate rather than confound understanding. (Bolster, 1983, pp. 305–306)

Bolster adds that in such embryonic research – for that is what partnership supervision essentially is – the relationship between teacher and academic is more about perception than about politics. Together they develop 'insights into problematic dimensions' of the classroom that might otherwise have been unavailable to either party. Thus, in a sense, the academic is moving into the pragmatic world of classroom knowledge-building, but bringing into it a perspective that strengthens the practitioner's frameworks for critical analysis. Each partner can learn from what the other has to offer. Awareness of our readiness in education to lock ourselves up in separate domains (ivory towers and chalk-face/coal-face/grass-roots dwellings), we see partnerships between experienced teachers and higher education tutors as a way of minimizing professional suspicion and developing a sense of shared professional concerns. And aware too of the speed with which new teachers are socialized into the traditional perspectives of the profession, we think it important to provide students in initial training with experiences that might help them to hold on to the intellectual excitement of learning.

Notes

1. This account is based on a study reported more fully in Rudduck and Sigsworth (1983 and 1985).
2. This account is based on a study by May and Sigsworth and reported in Rudduck (1982).

11 Ownership as the Basis of School Commitment to Change*

The movement that signalled teachers' commitment to enquiry and innovation, whether at the departmental or the whole-school level, was the school-based curriculum development movement. It grew and flourished in the wake of the curriculum reform movement of the 1970s, a movement that was supported and inspired neither by government nor by schools but by teams of curriculum developers of uncertain status, often attached to universities. The curriculum reform movement represented, in my view, a much more benign and educationally well-informed authority than that of the government's present programme of reforms. At its best, it offered schools ways of examining and thinking about the relationships between values, teaching and learning strategies, and the structures that govern access to knowledge and determine achievement. It offered frameworks for thinking and planning within which schools might confidently have developed their own curricula, matched to local conditions and needs. But opportunities and exemplars were often perceived as impositions and prescriptions, and the uptake of projects was in practice limited and partial (see Steadman *et al.*, 1980). As a reaction against the adoption of central projects, some schools gave their commitment to a new do-it-yourself brand of curriculum development. Undoubtedly, as Hargreaves says, achievements are real and significant in schools where 'thoughtful and enlightened' teachers and headteachers work together on the task of curriculum analysis and development. What should concern us, however, is the absence, in public accounts of school-centred innovation (s.c.i), 'of that scepticism and watchfulness among academics and practitioners which so strongly characterises the debate surrounding the centralizing tendency of curriculum change' (Hargreaves, 1982, p. 252). Hargreaves argues that 'the heavy skewing of discussion away from sharp and constructively critical analysis' of school-based and

---

*The original account on which this chapter is based was written jointly with Brian Wilcox, Sheffield LEA's Senior Chief Adviser. Alan Skelton, from the Division of Education, University of Sheffield, helped with the interviews. A full account has been written by Clough et al., 1989.

school-centred innovation has left us with a naive faith in its goodness. This faith may conceal serious misunderstandings about the reality of decision-making procedures and about the reality of the teacher autonomy that the movement celebrates, and, it is assumed, achieves.

For example, Hargreaves asks what 'active participation' by teachers in school-based or school-centred curriculum development really means, hinting that such popular but undefined terms might be largely symbolic. Their purpose, he suggests, is 'to arouse sympathy and support by localising s.c.i. within the cherished tenets of social democratic thought and practice' (ibid., p. 254). Hargreaves suggests that the concept of participation is being used as a legitimizing device for forms of social control, and in his concluding paragraphs he asks some sharp questions about the realities of the links between participation and democracy:

> Is "democracy" a realisable goal so long as heads retain final and long-standing responsibility for the decisions that are taken within schools? Can teachers reasonably be expected to participate in a democratic process of s.c.i. when the majority are excluded from other important centres of decision-making?

What, he asks, is the effect of both 'the relative exclusion of ordinary teachers from the wider governance of education, [and] their restricted access to educational theory?' What is required is close examination of the forms that participation takes when it is implemented in particular programmes of staff development and curriculum innovation:

> What needs to be adduced in particular is whether teacher participation leads them at present to being *in control* of the curriculum, or to remaining *in service* to ends formulated by others. (ibid., p. 255)

Accounts of s.c.i. in action have tended, according to Hargreaves (1982, p. 253), to be exhortatory (persuading people of its virtues), taxonomic (listing the forms it takes), or unanalytically reflective (testifying to its success in particular situations). We are in need of 'critical and empirically-grounded accounts of particular schemes and projects . . . [and] of the decision-making process and its effects on the perceptions, indeed on the motivation and morale, of those involved'.

This chapter is a step in that direction. It looks at some of the problems in the process of building a sense of shared ownership of the problems of change, and of the problems of changing. The observations are based not on the experience of a scatter of individual schools, which are exciting cultural islands of school-based curriculum development, but instead on the experience of teachers who were contributing to a programme of change across 36 secondary schools in one local education authority (i.e. school district). All the schools were involved in a programme designed to effect the radical transformation of the secondary curriculum. The local education authority (LEA), Sheffield, offered a broad framework of priorities (including the encouragement of active learning, the promotion of equal opportunities, the integration of curriculum experience) that allowed space for schools to maintain emphases that reflected their particular contexts and aspirations.

The scheme was distinguished by its bold vision. Sadly, circumstances largely beyond the control of the LEA made it difficult for the vision to be fully translated into practice. As Machiavelli said (according to Fullan, 1982, p. 88): 'Many have dreamed up republics and principalities which have never in truth been known to exist.' The energy of the scheme – which rested on successive teams of teachers being released from teaching for periods of up to a year – was diminished by drastic changes to the national financing of in-service. The interviews which this chapter draws on were undertaken during the first 15 months when the scheme was at its most buoyant and when optimism ran high. Evaluation data collected by others (Aspinwall, 1987a, b; Garforth, 1988; Pollard, 1987) are also drawn on. Our concern was to understand the potential and dynamic of working groups of teachers as they tried to build a common commitment to change, a shared understanding of the values that underpin change, and a reflective grasp of the process of school-wide change.

An important aspect of large-scale innovation of the kind attempted in Sheffield is the belief that schools *can* change and that teachers can be the agents of change. Money was spent not on paying 'experts' to come in and lead the task of change but, instead, to use Kanter's term, on 'grooming' the insiders to handle the responsibility themselves. Trust was rapidly built up through a ritualistic language, the rhetoric of 'ownership'.

The rhetoric of ownership

> The legitimising function of a reform can be understood by focusing on the nature of slogan systems. . . . A slogan works in education in a manner similar to the function of a slogan in the political world. A word . . . provides a way of symbolising the values and aspirations of a group. (Popkewitz *et al.*, 1982, p. xi)

The idea of 'ownership' quickly became a key term in the new language of change. It inspired 'collective confidence' (Fullan, 1982, p. 295); it made people feel that they were participating in worthwhile communal action. The term worked largely because it remained undefined. It had a good democratic ring to it and, like the term 'democracy' (Dunlop, 1979, p. 43), lacked any clear formulation, tending rather to be 'a hazy hugger-mugger of ideas and sentiments from which a man [*sic*] may draw consolation and the ease of a good conscience'. Our concern is not, therefore, to pin down meaning, for that would be to fragment the unity before its real foundation has been worked out and understood. What we can do is to look at some of the tensions or contra-dictions that the term has exposed in the hope that they may throw light on the complex and 'tantalising affair' of school improvement (Fullan, 1985, p. 391).

The issue of whether the initiative was 'owned' by the schools or by the LEA was not on the whole contentious. The framework for change offered by the LEA was accepted by most headteachers. Some justified their acceptance of the scheme to themselves and to others on the grounds that the initiative represented a set of social and moral imperatives for change (equal opportunities, active learning) that could not but be welcomed in all schools. Others projected *their* ownership of the initiative: 'The LEA is basing its policy on what *we* said *we* wanted for our schools.' As Fullan (1985, p. 403) observed, successful change processes can in fact combine elements that appear to be contradictory; for example, 'central initiative and direction' can be 'coupled with decentralized [school-based] analysis and decision-making'. In this case, 'ownership' was fairly legitimately claimed by both the LEA and its schools.

All heads promptly set about the task of identifying teachers to join the first pioneering teams and whole-school commissions that the teacher teams would work on during their period of release. The two local universities[1] whose teams of tutors were working closely with the seconded teachers were for a short time perceived as making a competitive 'ownership' bid. A tactical error occurred at the start of the year that highlighted their political threat: the LEA arranged for the teams of seconded teachers to go off to an intensive induction conference and their links with schools were temporarily severed. There was a flurry of anxiety. One teacher recalls his head's reaction – interestingly, blame was attributed not to the LEA who had organized the conference, but to the university where his team of secondees was based:

> Rumours circulated and our head, who is normally a very tolerant and fair man, said; 'I'm not having the University telling me what is happening here. These teachers are being taken out of schools and they are coming back as moles to overturn things.'

This suspicion that the universities might take over control of the process of change was soon allayed. We kept our promise that the teachers would spend only 2 days a week working with university tutors and would spend the other 3 days each week back in their schools. Thereafter, the university made strenuous efforts to maintain the trust of the headteachers: they were invited into each institution at intervals to participate in meetings that were set up exclusively for them as occasions when they could express their views and concerns and offer advice or criticism to the teams of tutors. Moreover, as the tutors started to work with the teams of seconded teachers in their schools, they came to be seen, on the whole, as supportive and sympathetic, rather than threatening.

In short, the battle for ownership was not played out between the LEA and the schools, as we might have anticipated, nor between the LEA and the universities, but between the teams of seconded teachers and their senior management; and, to a lesser extent, between the teams of seconded teachers and the majority of their colleagues who were not on release – those who remained 'back at the ranch', 'keeping the home fires burning', as some rather tartly described their role. The speed with which the initiative was launched exposed some weaknesses in the schools' capacity for communal planning. In some schools, the process of selecting teachers for a year of secondment – especially where 'volunteers' were rejected by senior management without the criteria of selection being made public – resulted in feelings of resentment towards those who were chosen. In very few schools were the tasks of defining commissions and selecting an appropriate team of teachers in fact handled in such a way that the whole staff felt from the outset a commitment to the enterprise as the first stage in a new and shared initiative for change (see Aspinwall, 1987b).

Ownership: The teachers and senior management

> What is not acknowledged in the literature [on teachers' resistance to innovation] is that "innovation" in education almost always implies reform initiated by upper management, consistent with its own managerial priorities, which is usually imposed on teachers with little or no prior consultation. (Carlson, 1986, p. 24)

As each team of teachers started their year of release, they were, in the main, collections of individuals from the same school rather than 'teams'. Most had had little opportunity in their day-to-day school life to explore each other's values and views of education (see Rudduck, 1986a). Some groups had a fairly coherent commission that allowed the members to begin to work as a team almost immediately, but others had individual tasks whose completion did not require close collaboration. The two universities, believing that a major precondition of change was the building of shared understanding and commitment, gave a lot of attention to the task of creating a sense of team, and made time formally available to the teams during their weekly 2 days of contact with them, to discuss strategies for change specific to their setting. Not all the teams saw such concerns as important in the early part of their period of release.

It took time to build a sense of real collaboration and trust and a readiness to look together at fundamental values and the hidden curriculum of secondary schooling. One constraint, apparent during the early part of the year, was senior management's increasing tendency to emphasize the secondees' accountability in terms of 'product' at the expense of 'process'. This was 'implicit power talk' (see Gordon, 1987, pp. 29–30), an assertion of 'ownership'. Management's concern, not unreasonably, was that the 'mission' be satisfactorily and speedily concluded, whether the goal was the drafting of a new timetable, a new syllabus, or a new integrated first-year programme. Control over the way secondees spent their time was exerted through an insistence on a tight delivery schedule: 'If we are to timetable for next year, we need the results.' Another strategy that minimized the power of the teams of teachers was to regard them as only one set of characters in a complex drama of change: 'There's a lot going on at this school that isn't anything to do with this particular initiative.' In such schools, the spotlight was made to play as much on the others as it did on the seconded teachers who, consequently, felt that their power to act was limited.

The secondees became aware of tensions: What *was* their relationship with senior management? Were they special? Were they privileged? The sessions offered by a visiting consultant on 'Handling the problems and process of change', where exchanges were made in total confidence, became the most sought after event and there was a waiting list to join! For the seconded teachers, the currency of process was gaining ground over the currency of product. By spring – the start of the final term of release – the urgency of their sense of product accountability had noticeably slackened, for by this time most had delivered what was crucial for next year's timetabling. But even as this physical and mental space to concentrate on process emerged, so it was cancelled out to some extent by the teachers' growing awareness of the reality of 'next year'. They started to realize that, despite the excitements and new learnings that release had yielded, they would probably return to the same positions in their schools, with the same status. Few were being consulted by senior management about the secondment plans for the second year of the initiative, and their experience was not being used to inform other curricular decisions. The headteachers were not, by and large, giving much attention to the re-integration of the seconded teachers, nor were they giving much prominence to the issue of continuity and liaison between the first year's and the second year's teacher teams. Few headteachers and senior management teams actually identified concrete strategies for sustaining the enthusiasm and influence of their change agent teams. Indeed, some headteachers may have chosen strategically not to make much of the return of the teacher teams.

The experience of the seconded teachers differed enormously, of course, from school to school and was clearly influenced by the micro-politics of individual settings. This variety was noted by Pollard (1987), a local headteacher, in his study of the ownership implications of the initiative. He identifies some broad categories for describing management's responses, with 'inertia' and 'positive infiltration' representing the two extremes. Management teams in the 'inertia' category tended 'to highlight the logistic problems of curriculum change' and the need to keep the school's team in check or even 'have their barmy ideas knocked on the head!' In some cases, of course, 'the blockage on . . . development could be traced to the inertia of the staffroom rather than to the intransigence of the headteachers', but it was senior management who, nevertheless, got the blame! At the other extreme were headteachers and senior management teams who supported the principle of 'positive infiltration'. Their strategies were characterized by 'open negotiation procedures which address the collective needs of the organisation'; here there was 'a feeling of trust between the hierarchy and the staff'. In these schools, secondees made 'considerable efforts' to make 'non-threatening presentations to the headteacher, the senior management team and staff', and senior management was more likely to provide guidance and counselling for their return. Although it is not clear from Pollard's account how many schools fall within this category, other evidence (Garforth, 1988) suggests that it is not many. This is perhaps not surprising, for, as Pollard observes, 'There has . . . been no overt attempt to . . . help support and guide site managers and their senior management teams.' This neglect occurred at a time, says Pollard, when the roles of management teams were 'increasingly susceptible' to a growing number of outside school forces which were challenging their authority 'to manage their own business'. Their sense of overall unease was not, therefore, surprising.

Ownership: The seconded teachers and their colleagues in schools

During the early months of their release the seconded teachers, sensitive to possible tensions with their colleagues back in school, tried presenting themselves in a service role, but as they became confident about the quality of their own insight and learning they inevitably wanted to take on leadership roles: 'It's taken half a year to realise that the task [of curriculum change] is about changing colleagues.' Ownership based on an understanding of the problem of change therefore became increasingly restricted to the few actually on release. They started to build up theories of local change that made them see themselves for a while as curriculum thinkers. But theorizing is not easily accepted in institutions where common values have not been explored at any depth and where the predominant climate is by and large hostile to theory. The seconded teachers had to prove themselves to their colleagues in the practical mode.

They anticipated that their colleagues would say to them what had been said in the past to teachers who returned from traditional one-year secondments: 'All right, clever clogs. You were out last year and now you're back. You can show us how it is done.' Although they were not 'out' for a whole year but were in fact in their schools for 3 days each week, they were not of course teaching on those 3 days and so were metaphorically 'out'.

The seconded teachers tried to empower their colleagues and to share ownership by encouraging more participation in school-wide discussion. Some tried to set up special occasions for the exchange of views and the analysis of practice. Others tried to modify the structure of conventional staff meetings so that more people could participate. The picture of conventional staff meetings that many painted was not one that readily supported the idea of communal 'ownership':

> Eventually, things come down to a staff meeting. The head does his best. He suggests what he wants to happen and then there's a strained silence because no-one else has been involved. So organisational trivia are paraded for half an hour. It's disastrous.

They tried talking with individuals before meetings, breaking down the formality of meetings by starting with coffee, or urging that colleagues, during the meeting, form smaller groups to discuss particular issues: 'We tried to get people together like human beings. I know that sounds desperate, but it's a big change.' But while they were working on new forms of meeting as a way of extending the sense of ownership to their colleagues, they were not always thinking about management's sensitivities:

> We held a meeting. I don't remember any occasion in the school where

ordinary staff have called a meeting. Our head was very uneasy. He came but he was very apprehensive and uptight. He thought things might get out of hand. We said: "Now look here. We do not want to subvert the existing order. Can't we make this new group a sub-group of the existing committee?"

Breakthroughs with staff discussion were not easy to sustain, and the conventional structures gradually came to reassert themselves – but with some loosening up of procedures that allowed the possibility of greater involvement by staff in the decision-making process. This, in many schools, was an important step in the move towards ownership of the problem of change.

Ownership: Post-secondment blues

As the year ended, for many seconded teachers it turned into a Cinderella experience: they had had their ball and at midnight the glass slippers vanished. This in itself may be one of the lessons of democratic ownership of change in schools: the commitment is to the empowering of the full complement of staff, not to the establishing of alternative, minority power groups.

When the secondees returned to their schools, they started to view their contribution to the change process more steadily and more phlegmatically. This shift of mood was partly a response to the realization that they had felt, to use an American term, 'downsized' (see Huberman and Miles, 1984). They said things like this: 'We are changing the world, shovelful by shovelful'; 'I'm not going to be a revolutionary, you know'; 'To do this is going to take us a little longer than we first imagined'; 'The big regret is that we couldn't achieve more in the time.'

The achievement of the first cohort of teachers was, as they came to see and accept, to lay the foundations for whole-school change, to get things going. In their stories about themselves, they changed from being the people who accomplish the change to the people who have given it a good start: 'We were the group that had to stop the ball rolling in the way it was going, look at it, and then get other people to look at it. That is the first stage'. They had to understand that change is a slow process and that the system was not ready to take full advantage of what they had to offer. They also had a sense of waste – some viewed it with understanding and a wise patience, and some with irritation: 'the unleashed energy that remains untapped, that frustrates me', said one secondee. 'You know, we're just back to where we were before – they've just accepted us back in as ourselves – i.e. as though *we* haven't changed at all', said another. The expected crowns of laurels either did not materialize, or, in some settings, turned out to be crowns of thorns. Personal commitment had to be very strong indeed to enable the pioneers, once back, to accept the heavy workload that they had to carry to ensure the continued interest of their colleagues: 'We're being given extra responsibility but no financial recognition.' Secondees also had to face the harsh fact that the tide of everyday pressures, 'other people's trivia', sometimes threatened to wash away the footsteps that seemed to be leading to change. One seconded teacher admitted to feeling as though he were 'drowning in a sea of demands' – 'completely devoured by the essential needs of day to day working'. Six months after their return, the contrast between the time to think during the year of secondment and the absence of time to think now that they were back 'in harness' was still a shock.

What helped secondees to maintain their sense of commitment? Not the continuity of dialogue with other members of their pioneering team, as it was only in a small minority of schools that they were given any extra time to reconvene as a group. The memory of things past remained a source of strength and there was an informal sense of bonding; and, significantly, many seconded teachers enrolled on part-time programmes of study that provided them, at the universities, with continuing opportunities to reflect on the experience of change.

The opportunities for learning that the year 2 teams had were in many ways restricted (few had a whole year of release). Many schools opted to release more teachers for a shorter time rather than fewer for a longer time. Ironically, this strategy accentuated the sense of involvement but may not have secured the same depth of understanding. At the end of their year of action and reflection, the first cohort of teachers had talked impressively not only about the new timetables, their new integrated courses and their new approaches to assessment, but also about the psychology of change:

> I think I'm more sensitive to the management of change, and attentive to the feelings involved.

> You've got to drag everyone else with you and if you don't drag them you're not going to get anywhere anyway. I think it's a process of talking to people and sharing your ideas with people and in the end coming back with something they can accept. . . . We [the secondees] don't have any real power . . . and you have to change people in the end in the way they want to change, so I suppose "dragging" people isn't quite the right metaphor.

These are hard-won insights into the realities of change. There is now, in many of the seconded teachers, a greater wisdom than when they were experiencing the manic optimism of their early pioneering days!

The significance of ownership

The aspiration towards a shared commitment to change is ambitious in the sense that the habits and structures that hold traditional values in place are not easily dismantled. For a conventional school staff, the ideology of separatism has to be replaced by one of collegiality. If the curriculum is to be coherently reshaped, then the criteria that inform judgement must be clarified and meanings assigned through collaborative effort. But as Bates (1987, p. 85) reminds us, the notions of culture lying behind such persuasions are often 'trivial, static and manipulative'. They are manipulative in the sense that the process of redefinition is likely to occur within the familiar framework of the managerial tradition, i.e. the new culture can be imposed from the top! Space needs to be made for political struggles over ideologies and commitments to be worked through. Most schools lack the conventions that would support a commitment to the kind of debate that Bates advocates which would 'enable the articulation and where possible the resolution of conflicts contained within the cultural politics of the school'. Management teams may need more support in developing a role that offers leadership in critical analysis and that is prepared to establish structures to support an informed dialectic focusing on issues of democracy and social justice (see Bates, 1987, p. 110).

Many secondees tried to take on the role of facilitating more open debate but they were, as we have seen, uncertain (especially after their return) about their right to act outside their own areas of formal responsibility, and they became increasingly reluctant to confront the question of their own power: 'I always get a bit uncomfortable about power. I know it exists'; 'I'd wriggle on the word power. We've been recognised for what we've been about – but power sounds threatening'; 'I'm anxious not to give an impression of being on an ego trip and forming a power base. I don't think it's at that level'; 'We haven't been a power group. We've worked within the structure because if we set ourselves up as important people – I don't think that will be the way of doing it.' But the power issue is important in schools and must be faced, as Kanter (1983, p. 18) reminds us from her study of innovation in industry:

> The degree to which the opportunity to use power effectively is granted or withheld from individuals is one operative difference between companies which stagnate and those which innovate.

The teachers who had pioneered the rolling programme of release had acquired a certain power-through-understanding but their power to act was constrained. The complexities of 'ownership', as they related to senior management and as they related to their non-seconded colleagues, led them, as they faced full-time return to their schools, either to deny or to disguise something of what they had learned. To the extent that they did this, the potential for fundamental change may have been diminished. Indeed, they talked about ownership increasingly in terms of their control of their *own* understanding and action and the sense of personal freedom that the year of secondment had given: 'Nobody's ever given me the chance before to say how I use my time'; 'After years of being programmed or the programmer of other people, freedom is unbelievable.' As Fullan (1982, p. 259) said:

> Teaching . . . suffers from the lack of opportunity that teachers have as individuals, and particularly in interaction with other teachers, to reflect, to observe, to discuss, to plan.

There is no doubt that many teachers, in their year of release, experienced excitement and a sense of mastery in attempting something new, but if, as Fullan (1982) suggests, it is the development of personal efficacy *and* collective confidence that is crucial in bringing about school change, then more attention must be given to the task of building structures that will enhance and sustain shared vision, shared understanding and collaborative effort.

Overall, the rhetoric of 'ownership' was a good rallying cry. As Popkewitz *et al.* (1982, p. 169) observe: 'all reform programmes feature rituals, ceremonies and particular language styles which create a feeling that things are getting better'. Reform is an act of social affirmation (ibid., p. 3), a way of helping people to rediscover and recommit themselves to ideals that can guide their thinking and shape their action but which have become sealed off and sedimented over by the narrow-focused habits of everyday survival. The rhetoric provided a language that most people could relate to and could quickly learn to speak – the actions had to come later.

Conclusion

At the start of the LEA's initiative, most schools had no way, either politically or procedurally, of arriving at a communal decision about the curriculum task that the seconded teachers were supposed to take on for their schools. An attempt was made to promote a democratic sense of the ownership of change without any prior attention being given to the task of helping senior management teams come to terms with the implications of such an aspiration.

Within the schools, the first cohort of seconded teachers, as they came to understand the complexities of the task of change and how power relations were at the heart of things, took on the role of liberators. It was their duty, in relation to their fellow teachers who were not on secondment, 'to restore the visions that had been muted by years of schooling' (Grumet, 1981, p. 122). Had they not had a full year of secondment they might not have moved beyond the basic requirement to deliver short-term products. The understandable unpreparedness of the system – the ambivalence of senior management towards the secondees' advocacy, and the resentment of colleagues who had not been chosen for secondment – put a brake on change but did not stop it.

The crucial achievement will be to find a way of 'hanging on to the initial magnitude of change in the midst of poor local fit and general system stress' (Huberman and Miles, 1984, p. 297). A common framework of meaning will be needed that is strong enough to unlock habit and influence action:

> The crux of change involves the development of meaning in relation to a new idea . . . but it is individuals who have to develop new meaning and these individuals are significant parts of a gigantic, loosely organised, complex, messy social system which contains myriad . . . worlds. (Fullan, 1982, p. 79)

That is the nature of the task in school-based and school-wide curriculum change. If the effort can be sustained, then one significant benefit will be that teachers in the participating schools could have what the fragmented intrusions of the curriculum development of the 1970s could not give: namely, insight into the task of facing and managing the continuous experience of change, including its strains and its internal politics.

Tangerud and Wallin (1986, p. 56) argue that very little school improvement can take place unless the existing power structure has been clearly analysed and a realistic strategy developed. In Sheffield, the analysis will have to follow on the heels of action, and the continuity of successive cycles of secondment may prove to be a good strategy for assisting with retrospective analysis and for supporting reflection-in-action – provided that the commitment continues to understanding the problem of change at district, institutional, group and individual levels.

Four years on from the start of the initiative, as the complexity of the undertaking has been exposed, the 'Alternative of Grandeur' strategy for innovation that the LEA and many of the first cohort of teachers were committed to has given way to the more measured 'Strategy of Gradualism' (see Smith *et al.*, 1986, pp. 275–6). The concern now is to keep the programme moving forward in a reasonably coherent array, to use reflection and analysis as a way of increasing everyone's understanding of the problem of change, and to invest in approaches that will steadily bring the action of change closer to the rhetoric of change.

Whether it will be possible to continue such large-scale collaborative efforts at change when the new national curriculum casts its shadow over secondary schools remains to be seen. In Sheffield, a sense of corporate power in the face of government interventions may well strengthen commitment to the local initiative. What matters, as progress must now be steady and purposeful, is how that commitment can be kept alive.

One could say that the story of the Sheffield initiative is of teachers who became potentially radical but who stepped back a little from the hard edge of change as they confronted the traditional authority structures of their institutions and the dilemmas of interpersonal power relationships. It is also a story of the difficulty of achieving rapid system-wide change. If overall change to the culture of schooling is to be seriously addressed, innovation needs to set a steady pace and sustain it through committed involvement and shared understanding.

PART 5

Taking Stock

12 Building and Sustaining Alternative Habits of Thought and Disposition

The task of schooling, as Ball (1988, pp. 292–3) points out,

> is increasingly subject to the logics of industrial production and market competition . . . technologies of control replace open ideological dispute. . . . Within such a discourse the curriculum becomes a delivery system and teachers become its technicians or operatives.

It all started, says Ball (1988, p. 289), with the publication of the first of the Black Papers in Education in 1969 by right-wing writers who blamed teachers for the radical adventuring of the curriculum development movement which, in their view, had resulted in falling academic standards and indiscipline. The criticisms were often contradictory, however, for while teachers were accused of being too progressive they were also accused, as the agenda changed, of clinging on to an academic curriculum that was ill-suited to contemporary needs and which fostered an anti-industrial ethos. The Great Debate of 1976 was stimulated by a deepening sense of national and economic decline – the responsibility for failure being largely attributed to schools. The view that radical solutions were required if economic disaster was to be averted amounted to an invitation for strong government intervention. And intervene it did! Because the Department of Education and Science was implicated in the blame attached to schools, the government could, with some legitimacy, set up a new agency (the Manpower Services Commission, now the Training Agency) to initiate curriculum reform through a new style of glossy categorical funding. The financial bait proved irresistible – schools and LEAs were hooked. The pressure was then extended and it culminated in the Education Reform Act of 1988. In the UK, we now have a new national curriculum framework, new attainment targets and testing programmes, new appraisal schemes for teachers, new patterns of local financial management, new powers for school governing bodies, and opportunities for schools to opt out of the state system. There will be more choice for parents, greater control of school governing bodies by non-professionals, and more emphasis on the inspection of schools. These things have a popular appeal which makes them impervious to rational criticism (see Homan, 1987, p. 15). The public is being carefully acclimatized to the idea of paying for education in a 'free market' situation, and the rhetoric of local financial responsibility and parental choice veils the spectre that local education authorities could, in time, be left to run only those schools which cater for 'children whose parents or guardians cannot afford to pay more than the minimum cost of education' (Demaine, 1988, p. 251). The state is using new structures of control to redefine the social purposes and outcomes of education. As Hargreaves and Reynolds (1989b, p. 2) have warned:

> We are entering a period of reduced state support for education overall, together with increasing state control over what remains . . . the vitality and sheer existence of state comprehensive education as we have come to know it is now in serious jeopardy.

Indeed, the two writers offer a gloomy prognostication of our educational future under the recent Education Reform Act. Reynolds suggests that:

> Education will henceforth exercise a reproductive rather than a transfor-mative function, re-enforcing traditional social, ethnic and gender divi-sions, rather than seeking to change them; . . .
>   . . . education will henceforth reassert academic goals rather than so-cial or personal goals; . . .
>   . . . opportunities for critique, both within courses of initial and inser-vice teacher education and in schools, will be diminished or dele-gitimised. (Reynolds, 1989, p. 192)

As university tutors, we could reject Reynolds's pessimism, reassert our trust in teachers, and put all our efforts into supporting them in the new imperatives for school reform – helping them to get on with and make the best of the task that government has set them. This approach could, if we were not wary, take us dangerously close to incorporation and loss of impetus to question and chal-lenge. Alternatively, we could offer sustained critique and opposition from outside, but, as David Hargreaves (1989, pp. 214–15) has warned, 'without alternative visions, critique deteriorates to mere criticism'. We could, of course, try to combine these two positions: it is probably important to make sure that we have '*usable* intellect and imagination (Silberman, 1970, p. 380) for we will need, at some level, to involve ourselves in the action: as intellectuals we must contribute more than our ideas to struggles for progressive social transformation' (Ginsburg, 1988, p. 365). A major responsibility for university staff is to try to sustain opportunities for dialogue, with teachers, about funda-mental values and issues. There are three arenas in which university staff can work with and offer support to teachers in schools: through in-service educa-tion, through pre-service education, and through research.

What of the potential of 'building and sustaining alternative habits of thought and disposition' through *in-service activities*? Carr (1986, p. 6) offers a powerful warning:

Any approach to teacher education which does not encourage teachers to reflect critically on their own educational views, and on the nature of education as it is realised in the institutional setting of schools, will be either inherently conservative or dangerously doctrinaire.

Sadly, the opportunities for extended professional study, where the habit of critical reflection is most likely to be encouraged in partnership with sympathetic university staff, have, in the UK at least, been disastrously reduced. Without such opportunities, teachers are likely to have difficulty committing themselves to sustained and coherent practice-related studies that have a critical and reflective edge. Instead, priority is being given to quick periods of release to allow teachers to fulfil short-term tasks. As Hargreaves and Reynolds (1989b, p. 23) have said: 'There is greater pressure towards productivity but reduced opportunity to reflect on the worth and rationality of what is being produced'. Teachers are increasingly denied space in which to engage in focused critical questioning. As Stenhouse (1984b, p. 75) warned: 'Improving education is not just about improving teaching as a delivery system.'

And what about the contribution of *initial teacher education* to the task of building alternative habits of thought and disposition? Giroux and McLaren (1987, p. 286) remind us that:

one of the great failures of North American education has been its inability seriously to threaten or eventually replace the prevailing paradigm of teacher as a formal classroom manager with the more emancipatory model of the teacher as critical theorist.

At the same time, they continue, 'teacher education has consistently failed to provide students with the means . . . for fashioning a more critical discourse and set of understandings around the goal and the purposes of schooling'. And, recently, John Wilson (1989, p. 5) has said that 'all practising teachers, right from the beginning, face problems both inside and outside the classroom which are not purely "practical" and involve serious reflection on educational and social issues'.

Teacher educators are not only being criticized by radical educators for not going far enough, they are also being criticized by the new right for going too far. New curriculum courses and perspectives – such as world studies and equal opportunities issues – have a dangerous edge, it is said, for they have often been nurtured by an 'inadequate and politically biased sociology' that has infiltrated the schools via programmes of initial teacher education (Hillgate Group, 1986, p. 5). It is 'unhealthy', argue members of the Hillgate Group, to help pupils respond to issues of race and equality for such concerns can 'destroy altogether the basis of our national culture'. Attempts to help young people think critically are dismissed as yielding merely 'an opinionated vagueness' (Hillgate Group, 1987, p. 3).

Teacher education programmes are now, in the main, planned and conducted in close partnership with teachers, and they are strongly school-centred and practice-focused. None the less, they are often dismissed (O'Hear, 1988,

1989; Anderson, 1988) for being too theoretical: O'Hear (1988) also argues that there are perfectly good teachers who have not undergone any formal training (ibid., p. 7) and that practical knowledge is best acquired through experience (ibid., p. 17). Such views have a superficial, popular appeal that makes them particularly potent at the present time.

There is considerable evidence to support the thesis (Hargreaves and Reynolds, 1989b) that the state has constructed and then exploited a view of schooling as a crisis of under-achievement. The same thing is happening in relation to teacher education. In the face of such a crisis, vocal groups can urge the state to accept a mandate for reform. The reform that O'Hear and fellow pamphleteers of the New Right propose is school-based, on-the-job training. Acceptance of the idea of on-the-job training (although not generally welcomed by the teacher unions), is made more palatable by a recognition of the desperate shortage of teachers in some areas of the country. The underlying concern may well be to remove teacher education from the 'dangerous' influence of the universities. But if new teachers are not actively helped, through their work with university tutors, to acquire 'new habits of thought and disposition', then their capacity to contribute to the task of achieving fundamental change in schools will be limited from the outset. As Lawn (1989, p. 148) recently stated: 'The idea of the reflective teacher is a crucial one for teacher education and stands in increasing relief to a limited vocational training which is [being] imposed on tutors and students.'

What of *teacher research* as a way of building and sustaining alternative habits of thought and disposition? The picture is not clear. We hear David Hargreaves (1984, p. 18) warning classroom practitioners against taking on a quasi-academic role as researchers, when 'in reality they cannot and should not want to imitate the professional researcher'. Rowland (1985, p. 26) elaborates on this position: what teachers can do is different from 'normal academic research', he argues. Teachers are in the privileged position of being better able than outsiders to interpret the thoughts and intentions of the children whom they teach: the point of classroom research (or 'enquiry' as he chooses to call it) is for teachers to understand, in some depth, more about the learning process. Others suggest that the more private, classroom-focused style of practitioner enquiry is not enough: '. . . the defect of the reflective approach is that it is severely constrained and limited by what it ignores' (Smyth, 1987a, p. 159). What it ignores are the wider social and political frameworks, beyond the classroom and the school, that shape the parameters of education in ways that teachers, with their eyes drawn to the minutiae of their own practice, too often fail to see. The distinctive feature of teacher enquiry, the individual struggling to understand the events and interactions of his or her own classroom, may not be a powerful force for change. Adelman and Carr (1988) spell out the weakness of the softer approach:

> by developing primarily as a form of teacher-controlled classroom research [it] has managed to create for itself the image of a popular "grass-roots" movement which neither threatens, nor is it self-threatened.

Such practitioner research, they say, can run the risk of addressing trivial questions, lacks cumulative power, and offers no collective, radical challenge – but on the other hand reflective, classroom-focused research is a way of building excitement, confidence and insight – and these are important foundations for career-long personal and professional development.

Where do teachers themselves stand in relation to these two models of research? Huberman (1989) offers an account of career 'stages' derived from a detailed analysis of interviews conducted with 160 Swiss teachers selected to form 'experience groups' (5–10 years, 11–19 years, 20–29 years and 30–39 years of experience). Teachers in the later stages of their career were presented as passing through a period of structural reform (such as many teachers are now facing in the UK) and entering a final phase of 'positive focusing', 'defensive focusing' or 'disenchantment'. Teachers in the 'defensive focusing group' are described as 'specialising; reducing commitments; using seniority to carve out a comfortable schedule; relating only to a small circle of peers'. They are the traditionalists who opposed educational innovation and 'were brought kicking and screaming through'. The 'disenchanted' are those who supported the idea of reform but who became disillusioned because the values had been undermined or confounded, and because administrators failed to carry through their support for the innovation and for the teachers engaged in the innovation. The teachers whom Huberman chooses to describe as 'positive focusers' ('narrow focusers' seems to me to be a more appropriate label) are described in the following two paragraphs:

> Put briefly: teachers who steered clear of . . . multiple classroom innovation, but who invested consistently in classroom-level experiments – what they called "tinkering" with new materials, different pupil grouping, small changes in grading systems . . . were more likely to be "satisfied" later on in their career than most others were and *far* more likely to be satisfied than their peers who had been heavily involved in school-wide or district-wide projects.
>
> So "tinkering", together with an early concern for instructional efficiency ("getting it down into a routine, getting the materials right for most situations I run into") was one of the strongest predictors of ultimate satisfaction. Inversely, heavy involvement in school-wide innovation was a fairly strong predictor of "disenchantment" after 20–25 years of teaching. Tending one's private garden, pedagogically speaking, seems to have more pay-off in the long haul than land reform, although the latter is perceived as stimulating and enriching while it is happening.

Huberman's analysis has some disturbing implications for those who are both interested in the more radical forms of teacher research and concerned to stem the current exodus from the profession of those who have become disenchanted. It seems, according to Huberman, that teachers are most satisfied by small modifications in the settings in which they work which allow them to take a different perspective on their work. His analysis would question the appropriateness of introducing teachers to research that reaches out beyond the walls of the classroom. Alternatively, Huberman's work might be perceived as emphasizing the need to encourage teachers to think more deeply about funda-mental values in their work, and to find satisfaction in a communal progress towards the realization of such values – in short, to commit themselves, as a school staff, to more radical change efforts where there is a clear, educationally justifiable, need for reform. Where Huberman takes the 'positive focusers' as his target group for preventive action, I would opt instead for the 'disen-chanted'. This is the group whose members had the visions and had identified the values that mattered to them as teachers but who had become disillusioned by lack of support. Our main concern should be to find ways of identifying such teachers – for they are in the system – and helping them to keep the visions and the values alive.

The need, as Carr (1986, p. 8) defines it, is to develop self-critical com-munities within which teachers can treat educational policies, practices and institutions as problematic. Our aim in universities would be to ensure that we as teacher educators are committed in our work to reflection on action and serious thought about values and purposes and that we continue to find ways of working with groups of teachers who are willing to endorse the significance of research, for research is the fundamental exemplar of the right to understand.

Of course, university staff are now subject, as are teachers in schools, to new systems of surveillance and control, inluding staff appraisal, and performance analysis is used as a basis for selective central funding. The threat of cut-backs in finance and staffing makes us vulnerable to market forces in the same way that schools now are, and the danger is that this vulnerability may make us cautious where earlier we would have been more courageously defiant. For example, we may be wary about how far to go in criticizing government policy, and yet that has been a traditional and important responsibility of the university. It seems to me that we must keep our courage and sustain our commitment to the rigorous analysis of educational policy. In particular, we have to place on our research agenda the determinants of the research process itself (see Lundgren, 1988, p. 18). This is a period in which administrators have consider-able power to decide what research is to be financed, and it is crucial that we understand what values are constraining or directing the focus of enquiry. Such research will enable us to see more clearly 'how knowledge *about* education is created and how a language *about* education is established' – in short, how research is currently endorsed 'by being "cogged" into the state apparatus' (Lundgren, 1988).

In troubled times it is up to the university in particular to help teachers build 'a language and a set of arguments with which they may defend' their commit-ment to 'the educational quality of teaching' (Carr, 1989b, p. 18). And we must make sure that all those who work in local partnerships to improve quality are able to go on speaking that language. The coherence and usefulness of such local partnerships between universities and schools will depend on the following:

- The readiness of the partners to give up their traditional mythologies about each other, and learn to respect each other's strengths.
- The building of a shared commitment to change, to exploring alternatives and to pushing back the limits of expectation in learning.
- The building of a shared commitment to clarifying values, principles and purposes, and to understanding the social and political contexts in which those values, principles and purposes are set to work.
- Recognition that the pace of worthwhile change – change that achieves new cultural coherence and significance – is relatively slow and that ways have to be found of keeping up the momentum.

These are not easy commitments. Gunnar Berg (1989, p. 58) has recently said that 'the basic condition of professionalization is that it must be sanctioned by the environment in which it is carried on'. The present scene in the UK is not one that readily supports such commitments, and schools and universities need to plan how best they can work together in a spirit of determination and common commitment.

References

Adelman, C. and Carr, W. (1988). Whatever happened to action research? Paper given at the British Educational Research Association Annual Conference, University of East Anglia.

Anderson, D. (1988). Summary and Preface. In A. O'Hear, *Who Teaches the Teachers?* Research Report no. 10, pp. 3–4. London: Social Affairs Unit.

Anderson, R. and Snyder, K. (1982). Why such an interest in clinical supervision? *Wingspan*, **1**(1), 1–10.

Aoki, T. (1984). Towards a reconceptualisation of curriculum implementation. In D. Hopkins and M. Wideen (eds), *Alternative Perspectives on School Improvement*, pp. 107–139. Lewes: Falmer Press.

Apple, M.W. (1975). Scientific interests and the nature of educational institutions. In W. Pinar (ed.), *Curriculum Theorising: The Reconceptualists*, pp. 120–30. Berkeley, Calif.: McCutchan.

Aronowitz, S. and Giroux, H. (1986). *Education Under Siege*. London: Routledge and Kegan Paul.

Aspinwall, K. (1985). A biographical approach to the professional development of teachers. Unpublished MEd dissertation, University of Sheffield.

Aspinwall, K. (1987a). *Some Responses of SFS Secondees to this Year's Programme*. Evaluation Report, City of Sheffield Education Department.

Aspinwall, K. (1987b). *A Climate for Change*. Evaluation Report, City of Sheffield Education Department.

Ball, S. (1988). Staff relations during the teachers' industrial action: Context, conflict and proletarianisation. *British Journal of Sociology of Education*, **9**(3), 289–306.

Bates, R.J. (1987). Corporate culture, schooling and educational administration. *Educational Administration Quarterly*, **23**(4), 79–115.

Becker, H.S. (1982). *Art Worlds*. Berkeley, Calif.: University of California Press.

Berg, G. (1989). Educational reform and teacher professionalism. *Journal of Curriculum Studies*, **21**(1), 53–60.

Berger, J. and Mohr, J. (1967). *A Fortunate Man*. London: Writers' and Readers' Cooperative.

Berlak, A. (1985). Back to basics: Liberating pedagogy and the liberal arts. Paper given at the American Educational Research Association Annual Conference, Chicago.

Bernstein, B. (1975). Class and pedagogies: Visible and invisible. In *Class, Codes and Control, Vol. 3: Towards a Theory of Educational Transmission*, 116–56. London: Routledge and Kegan Paul.

Blackmore, J. (1990). The text and context of vocationalism: Issues in post-compulsory curriculum in Australia since 1970. *Journal of Curriculum Studies*, **22**(2), 177–84.

Bolster, A.S. Jr (1983). Toward a more effective model of research in teaching. *Harvard Educational Review*, **53**(3), 294–308.

Bridges, D. (1979). *Education, Democracy and Discussion*. Windsor: NFER.

Brown, P. (1987). *Schooling Ordinary Kids: Inequality, Unemployment and the New Vocationalism*. London: Tavistock.

Bruner, J. (1986) *Actual Minds, Possible Worlds*. New York: Harvard University Press.

Carlson, D. (1986). Teachers, class, culture and the politics of schooling. *Interchange*, **17**(4), 17–36.

Carnoy, M. and Levin, H.M. (1985). *Schooling and Work in the Democratic State*. Stanford, Calif.: Stanford University Press.

Carr, W. (1980). The gap between theory and practice. *Journal of Further and Higher Education*, **4**(1), 60–69.

Carr, W. (1982). Treating the symptoms, neglecting the cause: Diagnosing the problem of theory and practice. *Journal of Further and Higher Education*, **6**(2), 19–29.

Carr, W. (1986). Recent developments in teacher education: A response. Paper presented at the Conference on Teacher Research and INSET, University of Ulster.

Carr, W. (ed.) (1989a). *Quality in Teaching: Arguments for a Reflective Profession*. Lewes: Falmer Press.

Carr, W. (1989b). Introduction: Understanding quality in teaching. In W. Carr (ed.) *Quality in Teaching: Arguments for a Reflective Profession*, pp. 1–18. Lewes: Falmer Press.

Carr, W. (1989c). Action research: Ten years on. *Journal of Curriculum Studies*, **21**(1), 85–90.

Clough, E., Aspinwall, K. and Gibbs, R. (eds) (1989). *Learning to Change: An LEA School-focused Initiative*. Lewes: Falmer Press.

Cogan, M.L. (1973). *Clinical Supervision*. Boston, Mass.: Houghton Mifflin.

Connell, R.W., Ashenden, D.J., Kessler, S. and Dowsett, G.W. (1982). *Making the Difference*. Sydney: Allen and Unwin.

Cowie, H. and Rudduck, J. (1988a). *Cooperative Group Work: An Overview*. Learning Together – Working Together, Vol. 1. London: BP Educational Service.

Cowie, H. and Rudduck, J. (1988b). *School and Classroom Studies*. Learning Together – Working Together, Vol. 2. London: BP Educational Service.

Cronbach, L.J. (1975). Beyond the two disciplines of scientific knowledge. *American Psychologist*, **30**, 116–27.

Cuban, L. (1987). Cultures of teaching: A puzzle. *Educational Administrative Quarterly*, **23**(4), 25–35.

Demaine, J. (1988). Teachers' work, curriculum and the new right. *British Journal of Sociology of Education*, **9**(3), 247–64.

Denscombe, M. (1980). Pupil strategies and the open classroom. In P. Woods (ed.), *Pupil Strategies: Explorations in the Sociology of the School*, pp. 50–73. London: Croom Helm.

Department of Education and Science (1985). *Better Schools*. London: HMSO.

Duchamp, M. (1962). A letter to Hans Richter. Quoted in E. Lucie Smith (1969). *Movements in Art Since 1945*. London: Thames and Hudson.

Dunlop, F. (1979). On the democratic organisation of schools. *Cambridge Journal of Education*, **9**(1), 43–54.

Durkheim, E. (1977). *The Evolution of Educational Thought*. London: Routledge and Kegan Paul.

Eliot, T.S. (1958). The love song of J. Alfred Prufrock. In *Collected Poems 1909–1935*. London: Faber and Faber.

Elliott, J. (1983). A curriculum for the study of human affairs: The contribution of the work of Lawrence Stenhouse. *Journal of Curriculum Studies*, **15**(2), 105–123.

Entwistle, N. (1981). Recent trends in research on learning in schools and universities. *Scottish Educational Review*, **13**(2), 112–21.

Fielding, M. (1973). Democracy in secondary schools: School councils and 'shared responsibility'. *Journal of Moral Education*, **2**(3), 221–32.

Fox, G. (1979). Teacher authority: Secondary education. In J. Rudduck (ed.), *Learning to Teach through Discussion*, pp. 6–7. Norwich: Centre for Applied Research in Education (CARE) Publications, University of East Anglia.

Fullan, M. (1982). *The Meaning of Educational Change*. Ontario: OISE Press.

Fullan, M. (1985). Change processes and strategies at the local level. *The Elementary School Journal*, **85**(3), 391–421.

Garforth, J.M. (1988). *Evaluation of the Sheffield Curriculum Initiative in Secondary Schools*. Evaluation Report, City of Sheffield Education Department.

Garver, E. (1984). The arts of the practical: Variations on a theme of Prometheus. *Curriculum Inquiry*, **14**(2), 165–82.

Ginsburg, M. (1988). Educators as workers and political actors in Britain and North America. *British Journal of Sociology of Education*, **9**(3), 359–67.

Giroux, H.A. (1981). *Ideology, Culture and the Process of Schooling*. Lewes: Falmer Press.

Giroux, H.A. (1983). *Theory and Resistance in Education*. London: Heinemann Educational.

Giroux, H.A. and McLaren, P. (1987). Teacher education as a counter public sphere: Notes towards a redefinition. In T.S. Popkewitz (ed.), *Critical Studies in Teacher Education*, pp. 266–97. Lewes: Falmer Press.

Goldhammer, R. (1969). *Clinical Supervision: Special Methods for the Supervision of Teachers*. New York: Holt, Rinehart and Winston.

Goodlad, J.I. (1984). *A Place Called School*. New York: McGraw-Hill.

Goodlad, J.I., Klein, M. and Associates (1970). *Behind the Classroom Door*. Ohio: Charles A. Jones.

Gordon, D. (1987). Autonomy is more than just the absence of external constraints. In N. Sabar, J. Rudduck and W. Reid (eds), *Partnership and Autonomy in School-based Curriculum Development*, pp. 29–36. Occasional Papers 10. Sheffield: University of Sheffield Division of Education (USDE).

Gottlieb, R.S. (1979). Habermas and critical reflective emancipation. In T.F. Geraets (ed.), *Rationality Training*. Ottawa: University of Ottawa Press.

Greene, M. (1973). *Teacher as Stranger*. Belmont, Calif.: Wadsworth.

Greene, M. (1985). Teacher as project: choice, perspective and the public space, mimeo.

Groundwater Smith, S. (1989). A process of critical enquiry: The evolution of curriculum knowledge in pre-service teacher education. Unpublished PhD thesis, University of Sydney.

Grumet, M. (1981). Restitution and reconstruction of educational experience: An autobiographical method for curriculum theory. In M. Lawn and L. Barton (eds), *Rethinking Curriculum Studies*, pp. 125–48. London: Croom Helm.

Hare, D. (1989). Cycles of hope and despair. *The Weekend Guardian*, June, pp. 3–4.

Hargreaves, A. (1982). The rhetoric of school-centred innovation. *Journal of Curriculum Studies*, **14**(3), 251–66.

Hargreaves, A. (1988). Teaching quality: A sociological analysis. *Journal of Curriculum Studies*, **20**(3), 211–31.

Hargreaves, A. and Reynolds, D. (eds) (1989a). *Education Policies: Controversies and Critiques*. Lewes: Falmer Press.

Hargreaves, A. and Reynolds, D. (1989b). Decomprehensivisation. In A. Hargreaves and D. Reynolds (eds), *Education Policies: Controversies and Critiques*, pp. 1–32. Lewes: Falmer Press.

Hargreaves, D. (1980). A sociological critique of individualism in education. *British Journal of Educational Studies*, **28**(3), 187–98.

Hargreaves, D. (1982). *The Challenge for the Comprehensive School*. London: Routledge and Kegan Paul.

Hargreaves, D. (1984). Introducing action enquiry. *Dialogue in Education*, **1**(1), 18.

Hargreaves, D. (1989). Educational policy and educational change: A local perspective. In A. Hargreaves and D. Reynolds (eds), *Education Policies: Controversies and Critiques*, pp. 213–17. Lewes: Falmer Press.

Hartley, D. (1986). Structural isomorphism and the management of consent in education. *Journal of Education Policy*, **1**(3), 229–37.

Hillgate Group (1986). *Whose Schools? A Radical Manifesto*. London: The Hillgate Press.

Hillgate Group (1987). *The Reform of British Education*. London: The Claridge Press.

Hinton, W. (1966). *Fanshen*. New York: Vintage Books.

Homan, R. (1987). The elimination of the local education authority. Paper given at the British Educational Research Association Annual Conference, Manchester.

Hopkins, D. and Wideen, M. (eds) (1984). *Alternative Perspectives on School Improvement*. Lewes: Falmer Press.

House, E.R. (1979). Technology versus craft: A ten year perspective on innovation. *Journal of Curriculum Studies*, **11**(1), 1–15.

Huberman, M. and Miles, M.B. (1984). *Innovation up Close: How School Improvement Works*. New York: Plenum Press.

Huberman, M. (1989). Teacher development and instructional mastery. Paper given at the International Conference on Teacher Development: Policies, Practices and Research, OISE, Ontario.

Hull, C. and Rudduck, J. (1981). *Pupils and Innovation*. Report to the SSRC, HR 6848/1.

Hull, C., Rudduck, J., Sigsworth, A. and Daymond, G. (1985). *A Room Full of Children Thinking*. Harlow: Longman/Schools Council.

Humanities Curriculum Project: An Introduction (1971). London: Heinemann Educational. (Revised by J. Rudduck, 1982, Norwich: School of Education Publications, University of East Anglia.)

Illich, I. (1981). *Shadow Work*. Boston: Marion Boyars.

Inglis, F. (1989). Theory and tyranny: The strange death of democratic England. *Cambridge Journal of Education*, **19**(2), 123–30.

Johnson, S.M. (1988). Schoolwork and its reform. *Journal of Education Policy*, **3**(5), 95–112.

Jonathan, R. (1987). Education under siege: The conservative, liberal and radical debate over schooling. *Journal of Curriculum Studies*, **19**(3), 567–9.

Joyce, B.R. and Clift, R. (1984). The phoenix agenda: Essential reform in teacher education. *Educational Research*, 5–18.

Joyce, B.R. and Showers, B. (1984). Transfer of training: The contribution of coaching. In D. Hopkins and M. Wideen (eds), *Alternative Perspectives on School Improvement*, pp. 77–87. Lewes: Falmer Press.

Joyce, B.R., Hersh, R.H. and McKibbin, M. (1983). *The Structure of School Improvement*. New York: Longman.

Kanter, R.M. (1983). *The Change Masters: Innovation and Entrepreneurship in the American Corporation*. New York: Simon and Schuster.

Lawn, M. (1989). Being caught in schoolwork: The possibilities of research in teachers' work. In W. Carr (ed.), *Quality in Teaching: Arguments for a Reflective Profession*, pp. 147–61. Lewes: Falmer Press.

Lundgren, U. (1988). 'Social engineering': Practical versus disciplinarian knowledge in Swedish post-war educational planning. *Studies of Higher Education and Research* (Newsletter of the Research on Higher Education Program, Sweden), **6**, 1–23.

McNeil, L. (1987). Talking about differences, teaching to sameness. *Journal of Curriculum Studies*, **19**(2), 105–122.

MacDonald, B. (1973). Briefing decision-makers. In D. Hamingson (ed.), *Towards Judgment*, pp. 12–30. Norwich: Centre for Applied Research in Education (CARE) Publications, University of East Anglia.

Marris, P. (1975). *Loss and Change*. New York: Anchor Press/Doubleday.

May, N. and Sigsworth, A. (1982). Teacher–outsider partnerships in the observation of classrooms. In Rudduck, J. (ed.) *Teachers in Partnership: Four Studies of In-service Collaboration*, pp. 43–56. London: Longman.

Meighan, R. (1989). *Flexi-schooling*. Ticknall: Education Now Publishing Cooperative.

Nias, J. (1984). Learning and acting the roles: In-school support for primary teachers. *Educational Review*, **36**(1), 3–15.

O'Hear, A. (1988). *Who Teaches the Teachers?* Research Report 10. London: Social Affairs Unit.

O'Hear, A. (1989). Teachers can become qualified in practice. *Guardian*, 24 January.

Olmsted, M.S. (1959). *The Small Group*. New York: Random House.

Page, R. (1989). The lower track curriculum at a 'heavenly' high school: Cycles of prejudice. *Journal of Curriculum Studies*, **21**(3), 197–221.

Perry, W.G. (1970). *Forms of Intellectual and Ethical Development in the College Years: A Scheme*. New York: Holt, Rinehart and Winston.

Polanyi, M. (1958). *Personal Knowledge*. London: Routledge and Kegan Paul.

Pollard, K. (1987). *The Management of New Teaching–Learning Styles in Secondary Schools*. Sheffield: Sheffield City Polytechnic, Department of Education Management.

Popkewitz, T.S., Tabachnick, R.B. and Wehlage, G. (1982). *The Myth of Educational Reform*. Madison: University of Wisconsin Press.

Popper, K.R. (1963). *Conjectures and Refutations*. London: Routledge and Kegal Paul.

Poppleton, P.K. (1988a). *Teacher Professional Satisfaction and its Implications for Secondary Education and Teacher Education*. ESRC Report, CO 925/0004.

Poppleton, P.K. (1988b). Teacher professional satisfaction: Its implications for secondary education and teacher education. *Cambridge Journal of Education*, **18**(1), 5–16.

Powell, A.G., Farrar, E. and Cohen, D.K. (1985). *The Shopping Mall High School*. Boston, Mass.: Houghton Mifflin.

Pratt, D. (1987). Curriculum design as humanistic technology. *Journal of Curriculum Studies*, **19**(2), 149–62.

Rae, J. (1973). On teaching independence. *New Statesman*, 21 September, p. 380.

Read, H. (1958). *Education through Art*. London: Faber and Faber.

Reynolds, D. (1989). Better Schools? In A. Hargreaves and D. Reynolds (eds), *Education Policies: Controversies and Critiques*, pp. 191–212. London: Falmer Press.

Rosario, J. (1986). Excellence, school culture and lessons in futility. *Journal of Curriculum Studies*, **18**(1), 31–44.

Rowland, S. (1985). Classroom enquiry: An approach to understanding children. *Dialogue in Education*, **1**(3), 26–8.

Rudduck, J. (ed.) (1979). *Learning to Teach through Discussion*. Norwich: Centre for Applied Research in Education (CARE) Publications, University of East Anglia.

Rudduck, J. (1981). *Making the Most of the Short In-service Course*. Schools Council Working Paper 71. London: Methuen.

Rudduck, J. (ed.) (1982). *Teachers in Partnership: Four Studies of In-service Collaboration*. London: Longman.

Rudduck, J. (1983). In-service courses for pupils as a basis for implementing curriculum change. *British Journal of In-service Education*, **10**(1), 32–42.

Rudduck, J. (1984a). Introducing innovation to pupils. In D. Hopkins and M. Wideen (eds), *Alternative Perspectives on School Improvement*, pp. 53–66. Lewes: Falmer Press.

Rudduck, J. (1984b). The 'hypothesis teacher' and the problem of helping children gain power through understanding. In B. Simon (ed.), *Margaret Gracie: A Teacher for Our Time*, pp. 15–24. Leicester: Forum Press.

Rudduck, J. (1985). The improvement of the art of teaching through research. *Cambridge Journal of Education*, **15**(3), 123–7.

Rudduck, J. (1986a). Curriculum change, management or meaning? *School Organisation*, **6**(1), 107–114.

Rudduck, J. (1986b). *Understanding Curriculum Change*. Occasional Paper 6. Sheffield: University of Sheffield Division of Education (USDE).

Rudduck, J. (1987). Partnership supervision as a basis for the professional development of teachers. In M. Wideen and I. Andrews (eds), *Staff Development for School Improvement*, pp. 129–41. Lewes: Falmer Press.

Rudduck, J. (1988a). Changing the world of the classroom by understanding it: A review of some aspects of the work of Lawrence Stenhouse. *Journal of Curriculum and Supervision*, **4**(1), 30–42.

Rudduck, J. (1988b). The onwership of change as a basis for teachers' professional learning. In J. Calderhead (ed.), *Teachers' Professional Learning*, pp. 205–22. Lewes: Falmer Press.

Rudduck, J. (1989a). Accrediting teacher education courses: The new criteria. In A. Hargreaves and D. Reynolds (eds), *Education Policies: Controversies and Critiques*, pp. 178–90. Lewes: Falmer Press.

Rudduck, J. (1989b). Practitioner research and programmes of initial teacher education. *Westminster Studies in Education*, **12**, 61–72.

Rudduck, J. and Hopkins, D. (1984). *The Sixth Form and Libraries: Problems of Access to Knowledge*. Library and Information Research Report 24. Boston Spa: British Library.

Rudduck, J. and Sigsworth, A. (1983). *Partnership: An Exploration of Student–Tutor Relationships in Teaching Practice*. Norwich: School of Education Publications, University of East Anglia.

Rudduck, J. and Sigsworth, A. (1985). Partnership supervision (or Goldhammer revisited). In D. Hopkins and K. Reid (eds), *Rethinking Teacher Education*, pp. 153–71. London: Croom Helm.

Rudduck, J. and Wilcox, B. (1988). Issues of ownership and partnership in school-centred innovation. *Research Papers in Education*, **3**(3), 157–79.

Runkel, P.J. (1984). Maintaining diversity in schools. In D. Hopkins and M. Wideen (eds), *Alternative Perspectives on School Improvement*, pp. 167–87. Lewes: Falmer Press.

Sarason, S.B. (1982). *The Culture of the School and the Problem of Change*, 2nd edn. Boston: Allyn and Bacon.

Scheffler, I. (1968). University scholarship and the education of teachers. *Teachers' College Record*, **70**(1), 1–12.

Schon, D.A. (1983). *The Reflective Practitioner*. London: Temple Smith.

Schon, D.A. (1987). *Educating the Reflective Practitioner*. San Francisco: Jossey Bass.

Schools Council (1965). *Raising the School Leaving Age*. Working Paper 2. London: HMSO.

Schools Council (1968). *Enquiry 1: The Young School Leaver*. London: HMSO.

Schwab, J.J. (1956). Science and civil discourse: The uses of diversity. *Journal of General Education*, 132–143. Reprinted in J. Westbury and N.J. Wilkof (eds) (1978). *Joseph J. Schwab: Selected Essays*. Chicago: University of Chicago Press.

Schwab, J.J. (1970). The practical: A language for curriculum. Paper given at the American Educational Research Association Annual Conference and printed by the Centre for the Study of Instruction. Reprinted in J. Westbury and N.J. Wilkof (eds) (1978). *Joseph J. Schwab: Selected Essays*. Chicago: University of Chicago Press.

Seifert, J. (1983). *An Umbrella from Piccadilly* (translated by E. Osers). London: London Magazine Editions.

Silberman, C.E. (1970). *Crisis in the Classroom: The Remaking of American Education*. New York: Vintage Books.

Slaughter, R.A. (1989). Cultural reconstruction in the post-modern world. *Journal of Curriculum Studies*, **21**(3), 255–70.

Smith, L.M., Kleine, P.F., Prunty, J.P. and Dwyer, D.C. (1986). *Educational Innovators: Then and Now*. Lewes: Falmer Press.

Smyth, W.J. (1985). Developing a critical practice of clinical supervision. *Journal of Curriculum Studies*, **17**(1), 1–15.

Smyth, W.J. (1987a). Transforming teaching through intellectualizing the work of teachers. In J. Smyth (ed.), *Educating Teachers*, 155–68. Lewes: Falmer Press.

Smyth, W.J. (1987b). *A Rationale for Teachers' Critical Pedagogy: A Handbook*. Victoria: Deakin University Press.

Squirrell, G., Gilroy, P., Jones, D. and Rudduck, J. (1990). *Acquiring Knowledge in Initial Teacher Education: Reading, Writing, Practice and the PGCE Course*. Library and Information Research Report 79. London: British Library.

Stake, R.E. (1987). An evolutionary view of programming staff development. In M. Wideen and I. Andrews (eds), *Staff Development for School Improvement*, pp. 55–69. Lewes: Falmer Press.

Steadman, S.D. and Parsons, C. (1980). *The Impact and Take-up Project*. Second Interim Report. London: Schools Council.

Stenhouse, L. (1963). A cultural approach to the sociology of the curriculum. *Pedagogisk Forskning*, Nordisk Tidsskrift for Pedagogik, pp. 120–34.

Stenhouse, L. (1979). Using research means doing research. In H. Dahl, A. Lysne and P. Rand (eds), *Pedagogikkens Sokelys: Festskrift til Johannes Sandven*, pp. 71–82. Oslo: Universitets Forlaget.

Stenhouse, L. (1980a). Curriculum and the quality of schooling. Paper given at Goldsmith's College Annual Conference and published in the *Conference Proceedings*.

Stenhouse, L. (1980b). Curriculum research and the art of the teacher. *Curriculum*, **1**(1), 40–44.

Stenhouse, L. (1980c) Product or process? A reply to Brian Crittenden. *New Education*, **2**(1), 137–40.

Stenhouse, L. (1983a). The aims of the secondary school. In *Authority, Education and Emancipation*, pp. 153–5. London: Heinemann Educational.

Stenhouse, L. (1983b). Towards a vernacular humanism. In *Authority, Education and Emancipation*, pp. 163–77. London: Heinemann Educational.

Stenhouse, L. (1983c). Research as a basis for teaching. In *Authority, Education and Emancipation*, pp. 177–95. London: Heinemann Educational.

Stenhouse, L. (1984a). A note on case study and educational practice. In R.G. Burgess (ed.), *Field Methods in the Study of Education*, pp. 263–71. Lewes: Falmer Press.

Stenhouse, L. (1984b). Artistry and teaching: The teacher as the focus of research and development. In D. Hopkins and M. Wideen (eds), *Alternative Perspectives On School Improvement*, pp. 67–76. Lewes: Falmer Press.

Stenhouse, L. (1984c). Evaluating curriculum evaluation. In C. Adelman (ed.), *The Problems and Ethics of Educational Evaluation*, pp. 77–86. London: Croom Helm.

Stenhouse, L., Verma, G.K., Wild, R.D. and Nixon, J. (1982). *Teaching about Race Relations: Problems and Effects*. London: Routledge and Kegan Paul.

Strauss, A. (1977). *Mirrors and Masks: The Search for Identity*. London: Martin Robertson.

Sultana, R.G. (1989). Transition education, student contestation and the production of meaning: Possibilities and limitations of resistance theory. *British Journal of Sociology of Education*, **10**(3), 287–309.

Tangerud, H. and Wallin, E. (1986). Values and contextual factors in school improvement. *Journal of Curriculum Studies*, **18**(1), 45–61.

Taylor, M. (1968). *The World and the American Teacher*. Washington DC: The American Association of Colleges of Teacher Education.

Toffler, A. (1970). *Future Shock*. New York: Bantam Books.

Toogood, P. (1989). Learning to own knowledge. In C. Harber and R. Meighan (eds), *The Democratic School*, pp. 98–121. Ticknall: Education Now Publishing Cooperative.

Watson, G. (1973). Resistance to change. In G. Zaltman (ed.), *Processes and Phenomena of Social Change*. New York: John Wiley.

Westbury, J. and Wilkof, N.J. (eds) (1978). *J.J. Schwab: Science, Curriculum and Liberal Education: Selected Essays*. Chicago: University of Chicago Press.

Wideen, M.F. (1987) Perspective on staff development. In M. Wideen and I. Andrews (eds), *Staff Development for School Improvement*, pp. 1–15. Lewes: Falmer Press.

Wilson, J. (1989). Authority, teacher education and educational studies. *Cambridge Journal of Education*, **19**(1), 5–12.

Withall, J. and Wood, F. (1979). Taking the threat out of classroom observation and feedback. *Journal of Teacher Education*, **30**, 1.

Wood, D. (1988). *How Children Think and Learn*. Oxford: Blackwell.

Woods, P. (ed.) (1980). *Pupil Strategies: Expectations in the Sociology of the School*. London: Croom Helm.

Woods, P. (1985). Conversations with teachers: Some aspects of life history method. *British Educational Research Journal*, **11**(1), 13–26.

Name Index

Subject Index